Living with Siva

Hinduism's Nandinatha Sutras

Sivaya
Subramuniyaswami

Published by
Himalayan Academy
California • Hawaii

First Edition

 Designed, typeset and illustrated by the swamis of the Saiva Siddhanta Yoga Order and published by Himalayan Academy, 1819 Second Street, Concord, California 94519.

Published by
Himalayan Academy
California • Hawaii

PRINTED IN USA

Dedication

THESE NANDINATHA SUTRAS WERE WRITTEN FOR THE BENEFIT OF THE HIGHEST ATTAINMENT, PARASIVAM, FOR ALL MY FOLLOWERS on this fourteenth day of March, 1991, the twenty-seventh anniversary of the mahasamadhi of my Satguru, Sage Yogaswami. We dedicate this proclamation to him and to all who preceded him in the holy Kailasa Parampara. We have received the blessings and authorization from Lord Ganesha to proceed at a very special time in a very special way. We have received the power, the lightening flash, from Lord Muruga and His permission to proceed. May all of humanity eventually see that our Supreme God Siva—creator, preserver and destroyer of all that is good, bad, confused and indifferent, the source of grace, the author of dharma, the giver of all good things, the light and love of the world—has always, does always, will always spread His goodness and glory everywhere.

Contents

Author's Introduction ix

PART ONE: ETHICS

1 The Purpose of Life.......................... page 3
2 Facing Life's Challenges 5
3 Yoga in Action...7
4 The True Values of Life 9
5 Yamas: Ten Classical Restraints..................11
6 Niyamas: Ten Classical Observances 13
7 Ahimsa, the Foremost Discipline..................15
8 Regrettable Exceptions to Ahimsa................17
9 Reverence for the Environment 19
10 Self Control 21
11 Regarding Worldly Activities.....................23

PART TWO: BELIEF

12 Authorized Scriptures..............................27
13 The Nature of God 29
14 The Nature of Souls and World 31
15 Karma, Evil and Wisdom...........................33

PART THREE: PRACTICE

16 Temple Worship......................................37
17 Cultural Accomplishments.........................39
18 Spiritual Study 41
19 Occultism 43
20 Spiritual Disciplines.................................45
21 Personal Disciplines.................................47
22 Symbols, Names and Mantras.....................49

PART FOUR: PERSONAL LIFE

23 Diet and Food....53
24 Health and Exercise....55
25 Tobacco and Drugs....57
26 Guidelines Regarding Alcohol....59
27 The Four Stages of Life....61
28 Approaching Death....63
29 About Death's Aftermath....65

PART FIVE: LIVELIHOOD

30 About Wealth....69
31 God's Money....71
32 Politics and Vocation....73
33 Instructions for Parliamentarians....75
34 Instructions for Scientists....77

PART SIX: MEN AND WOMEN

35 Instructions for Men....81
36 Instructions for Husbands....83
37 Instructions for Women....85
38 Instructions for Wives....87
39 Instructions for the Widowed....89
40 Instructions for the Single....91

PART SEVEN: THE FAMILY

41 Hospitality....95
42 Household Ethics....97
43 Raising Children....99
44 Preserving Family Unity....101
45 Preparing Youth for Adult Life....103
46 Duties of Young Adults....105
47 Arranging Marriages....107
48 Sustaining Marriages....109
49 About Divorce....111

PART EIGHT: PROTOCOL

50 Devotion to the Satguru 115
51 Working with the Satguru........................ 117
52 In the Satguru's Presence........................ 119
53 Respecting Saints and Dignitaries............... 121
54 Social Injunctions................................ 123
55 Interfaith Harmony.............................. 125
56 Avoiding Alien Influences....................... 127

PART NINE: THE FELLOWSHIP

57 Temples and Priesthood 131
58 Weekly Gatherings............................... 133
59 Guidelines for Business 135
60 New Followers 137
61 Conversion to Saivism 139
62 Adversaries and Detractors 141
63 Raising Sons for the Monastery 143

PART TEN: THE MONASTICS

64 Monastic Holy Orders 147
65 Monastic Mission................................ 149
66 Monastic Spirit 151
67 Monastic Attitudes.............................. 153
68 Monastic Personal Care.......................... 155
69 Monastic Travel and Retreat 157
70 Monastic Restrictions............................ 159
71 Monastics and the World 161
72 Instructions for Swamis......................... 163
73 Instructions for Achariyas 165

Conclusion...................................... 167
Glossary xvii
Index xxvii

Author's Introduction

MOST PEOPLE THINK OF THEMSELVES AS REMOTE FROM GOD, BUT THE HIGHEST SOULS ARE LIVING WITH HIM EVERY DAY, no matter what they are doing. They are living with Siva while working, while driving or performing ordinary chores. Siva is, for these remarkable devotees, closer than their breath, nearer than their hands and feet. They know that the only true happiness, the only permanent joy, comes from the Self. This is the true spiritual life, which recognizes that there is nothing that is not Siva.

From a psychological point of view, when the subconscious is at odds with soul qualities, with the basic laws of how we intuitively know what we should be doing, when the past of unsoulful deeds carries into the present, we are not able to live with Siva. Instead, we are living with humans, living with problems, living with the conflicting forces of the world.

Living with Siva is Siva consciousness. The reconciled past releases consciousness into the eternal moment in which we see Siva as the life and light within everyone's eyes. Living with Siva is living with everyone—every reptile, fish, fowl, animal and creature to the very smallest—in a consciousness of the one life force within all of them that sustains this perfect universe. Truly, God Siva is everywhere. He is the energy within our mind manifesting thought. He is the thought thus made manifest. He is the light within your eyes and the feel within your fingers. God Siva is the ignorance which makes the One seem as two. He is the karma, which is the law of cause and effect, and He is the maya, which is the substance of evolution in which we become so deeply immersed that we look upon the outside world as more real than God. God Siva is all this and more. He is the sun, the earth and the spaces between. He is the revealed scriptures and those who have scribed the scriptures. He is all who seek the wisdom of scripture, too. He dances in the atoms throughout this universe. He dances energetically, eternally. He is eternal movement. His mind is all-pervasive, and thus He sees and knows everything in all spheres simultaneously and without effort. He is the Self, and He is the energy we put forth to know the Self. He is the mystery which makes us see Him as separate from us. He is the energy of life, the power in the wind. He is the dissolution called death, the peace of motionless air. He is the great force of the ocean and the stillness on a calm lake. He is All and in all, our great God Siva, beyond time, beyond space, beyond form and form's creation, and yet He uses time and causes form. He is in the sky, in the clouds, in the swirling galaxies. His cosmic dance of creation, preservation and dissolution is happening this very moment in every atom of the cosmos. He is immanent, with a beautiful human-like form which can actually be seen and has been seen by many mystics in visions. He is also transcendent, beyond time, cause and space. Such are the mysteries of Siva's being.

At this time in the Kali Yuga, ignorance is equally distributed worldwide, and wisdom has become an endangered species. People are confused as to the performance of their duties, and too often duty is no longer even taught. Our scriptures are misinterpreted to justify actions that inflict injuries on humans and creatures alike. It is to liberate my followers from this confusion that these sutras have been written.

Forbearance, tolerance and compassion are not as popular today as they once were and perhaps may be at some future time when the darkness of ignorance is removed from the hearts of all people. Therefore, these sutras, translated into many languages for followers living in various countries, will play an important part in bringing the best of traditional Hinduism forward.

What you will read in *Living with Siva* describes how people lived and interrelated with one another in the days when love and peace, respect and wisdom prevailed. There is no new knowledge contained herein. Each sutra proclaims an ancient wisdom and protocol which, when followed, brings that same peace, harmony and refinement of enduring relationships into your life. Each of these 365 sutras, one to be read each day of the year, is a thread of purity, most from the historic past into the present, some from contemporary times. Even today, as we approach the 21st century, these precepts define the daily life of hundreds of millions of well-bred and well-raised Asian people.

Many who read these sutras will wonder to themselves, or even among friends, "Why do we need to follow such strict traditions and disciplines? Aren't they a little bit old-fashioned?" My Satguru, Sage Yogaswami, was asked these very questions half a century ago in Sri Lanka. He answered simply, "The railway engine pulls many coaches. Can it do so if it runs off the track? No. Great people have shown the path. We must follow it." Though challenging, the disciplines and guidelines described here create happy individuals, harmonious families and secure nations.

Sage Yogaswami made still another observation which points to the first reason for these sutras: "Because of worldliness, the light in the faces of the young has become less bright these days. The way is very long, and you must go forward slowly, keeping to the path, not walking on the thorns by its sides." These sutras define the path and the thorns that lie on either side of it.

There is a second reason for these sutras. When you take them as a total whole, you will glimpse the ideal community. Such a community is able to work together, love together, trust together, create together, serve Siva together, worship together, live together in a productive harmony, an ongoing creativity, as they each experience birth, life, death and birth again.

Thirdly, our followers have spread throughout the world, relocating themselves because of ethnic disputes, violence and economic deprivation within their homelands. Because of this diaspora, it has become necessary to restate the law of the culture, the protocol and modes of behavior that their forefathers knew and lived so well.

At this trying time in the history of my followers, these *Nandinatha Sutras* came forth as a boon from the Gods. In the seriousness of their search, followers were asking for advice and guidance as to how they should behave with one another, how they should relate and interrelate with their Satguru, achariyas, swamis, yogis and sadhakas, brahmacharis and brahmacharinis, husbands and wives, children, widows, widowers, divorcees and divorcés.

You will notice that about one seventh of the sutras are addressed to my monastics. It is important that families understand my expectations for the monastics and the other way around. It is the balance between the monastic community and the family community that stabilizes spiritual life in the physical world, in matters of marriage, business, politics, money and health. It is this same balance that creates a pleasant, ongoing, productive foundation for the upcoming generation.

I have written these sutras in simple English so that they can easily be translated and unambiguously understood. A small glossary has been prepared to define the few Sanskrit and Tamil words for which there were no satisfactory English equivalents and to provide a ready reference to the meanings of certain words for readers for whom English is a second language.

However, obscurities in such matters do arise, and this will also happen with these sutras. They shall be enforced and simply explained by my order of swamis, by councils on ministries and elders. But all final interpretations, clarifications, deductions, apparent contradictions, disputes and unraveling of subtle questions shall be made only by myself and my swami achariyas of our order. These achariyas are duly ordained and authorized by me to give interpretations of these sutras. While I live, my word shall be absolutely final. Future Satgurus after my mahasamadhi will progress the understanding of these precepts from century to century, language to language, forever and ever.

And now I shall address my followers who have become acquainted with me through dreams, visions, publications, lectures, personal encounters and hearing of me from others. I challenge you to boldly go forth in your spiritual quest. These 365 sutras give the protocol and practices as well as the attainments—the end in view. Within the pages of *Living with Siva* are restraints, encouragement, admonitions, enlightened coaching, even reprimands. There is much nourishment here for the intelligent soul who is pushing forward into peace and tranquility, having conquered the trials and tribulations of the yesterdays.

Study these sutras that I have unfolded and adjust your lives accordingly. Be unwavering in your commitment. You know the rightness of these guidelines for good conduct in your heart of hearts, soul of soul. Your inner ear hears and your inner eye sees the truth of each of these quatrains. To adjust your life to their wisdom is the discipline toward being able to come close to and then finally live with Siva. Of course, now, as in ages past, there are those dedicated to being nonconformist, committed to noncommitment, who discipline themselves to avoid a disciplined life. This book may confound them, for they do not understand discipline's place on the spiritual path. My followers are tolerant of less disciplined souls.

In the final analysis, it is up to each individual to cultivate soul qualities that are already resident within. This is done in a way similar to how a garden is nurtured along into bud, blossom and beauty. The weeds and harmful insects must somehow be kept away. There must be proper light and shade, water and sun. When conditions are right, the intended results manifest on their own. The laws within the *Nandinatha Sutras* are similar to what a gardener needs to know to raise his plant successfully, for the soul is a bud that blossoms, blooms and shines out its beauty, but only if the conditions are right.

Proceed with confidence. Don't look back. Fear not what others say or do. There is a new world tomorrow, and you are a vital part of it. The yesterdays cannot be adjusted or corrected, until we meet them with a new attitude born of knowledge and wisdom in the tomorrows of our future. We are bound together by bands of steel, as are all worshipers of Lord Siva. Following the protocol found in these sutras will keep this bondage happy and rewarding, thus avoiding the tugs and pulls of impropriety, thus averting the pitfalls of humanness which can so often bring pain and remorse.

We feel that anyone of any culture, creed or belief can benefit from reading *Living with Siva*, and will in their heart of hearts recognize the valid wisdom of these laws that have matured through the millennia.

Part One

Ethics

The Purpose of Life

SUTRA 1

All my followers shall strive for God-Realization as the first and foremost goal of life. They learn to dance with Siva, live with Siva, merge with Siva. Deep within they find their eternal, immortal oneness with God. Aum.

SUTRA 2

My followers must remember that the purpose of life is to wholeheartedly serve God, Gods and guru and fulfill the four traditional goals of duty, wealth, love and Liberation. Yea, they are servants of the divine. Aum.

SUTRA 3

My followers shall bask contentedly in Siva consciousness, seeing the pure life energy in every person, animal, bird, reptile, fish, insect, plant and tree, and even microscopic intelligence as being God Siva Himself. Aum.

SUTRA 4

All my followers should strive to be inwardly one with their Satguru, acknowledging the paramount need for a preceptor to guide them on the upward climb, the straight path that leads to Lord Siva's holy feet. Aum.

SUTRA 5

All my followers heed the ancient wisdom: "The physical body does not last forever. Age prowls like a leopard. Before the limbs lose their vitality, one should take to the auspicious path to the Self." Aum Namasivaya.

Facing Life's Challenges

SUTRA 6

All my followers shall cultivate a contemplative nature by meditating daily, seeking the light, drawing the lesson from each experience and identifying with infinite intelligence, not with body, emotion or intellect. Aum.

SUTRA 7

My followers accept as their own karma all experiences that come, however harsh or difficult, never uttering a syllable of complaint. Theirs is the power of surrender, accepting what is as it is, not as they want it to be. Aum.

SUTRA 8

All my followers live vibrantly in the eternity of the moment and flow with the river of life by giving up negative attachments, releasing the pains, injustices, fears and regrets that bind consciousness in the past. Aum.

SUTRA 9

My followers approach each enterprise with deliberate thoughtfulness, and act only after careful consideration. They succeed in every undertaking by having a clear purpose, a wise plan, persistence and push. Aum.

SUTRA 10

All my followers shall, by remaining steadfast on the spiritual path and relying on their indomitable will, righteously move the forces of the material world and not be moved or affected by them. Aum Namasivaya.

Yoga in Action

SUTRA 11

All my followers shall fulfill life's purposes by placing heavy demands on themselves from within themselves, never shirking their duties to their religion, family, community or planet. Yea, they are the lion-hearted. Aum.

SUTRA 12

All my followers must endeavor to be the best in whatever they do, excel and make a difference. However, they should remain apart from the demeaning and contentious "winners and losers" spirit of competition. Aum.

SUTRA 13

All my followers shall fulfill the five classical duties: virtuous conduct, daily worship and study, holy days, sacraments and yearly pilgrimage. Of strong will and clear conscience, they are unwavering on the path. Aum.

SUTRA 14

All my followers cultivate a love of learning and work diligently to personally guide their children's spiritual and secular education, especially in the early years. They must never proclaim, "I have learned enough." Aum.

SUTRA 15

All my followers should be instruments of peace wherever they are, preaching harmony in the midst of disharmony and finding agreement when others can only disagree. Yea, they are all peacemakers. Aum Namasivaya.

The True Values of Life

SUTRA 16

My followers shall render to those in need help which is loving, selfless and free from all expectation of repayment. They live in constant gratitude for all they have, never complaining about what they don't possess. Aum.

SUTRA 17

All my followers are honorable, cheerful, modest and full of natural courtesy. Having removed the darkness of anger, fear, jealousy and contempt for others, their faces radiate the kindly compassion of their soul. Aum.

SUTRA 18

My followers live with God Siva, close to His mystery. While others seek "name and fame, women and gold," they seek the clear white light within, find refuge in the stillness and hold Truth in the palm of their hand. Aum.

SUTRA 19

My followers keep the mountaintop perspective that life on earth is an opportunity for spiritual progress. They never lose sight of this wisdom by becoming infatuated with instinctive and intellectual pursuits. Aum.

SUTRA 20

All my followers know the great power of thought and desire, and thus choose theirs wisely. They know, too, the infinitely greater power of those who conquer desire by desiring only to know God. Aum Namasivaya.

Yamas: Ten Classical Restraints

SUTRA 21

All my followers shall practice the ethical restraint of noninjury, not harming others by thought, word or deed—even in their dreams. All adhere to truthfulness, refraining from lying and betraying promises. Aum.

SUTRA 22

All my followers shall uphold the virtue of nonstealing, neither thieving nor coveting nor entering into debt. All shall practice sexual purity, controlling lust by remaining celibate when single and faithful in marriage. Aum.

SUTRA 23

All my followers shall exercise patience, restraining intolerance with people and impatience with circumstances. All foster steadfastness, overcoming nonperseverance, fear, indecision and changeableness. Aum.

SUTRA 24

All my followers shall practice compassion, conquering callous, cruel and insensitive feelings toward all beings. All maintain honesty, vowing to renounce deception and wrongdoing. Yea, they are peerless in virtue. Aum.

SUTRA 25

All my followers shall be moderate in appetite, neither eating too much nor consuming meat, fish, shellfish, fowl or eggs. All uphold the ethic of purity, avoiding impurity in body, mind and speech. Aum Namasivaya.

Niyamas: Ten Classical Observances

SUTRA 26

All my followers shall allow themselves the expression of remorse, being modest and showing shame for misdeeds. All nurture contentment, seeking joy and serenity in life. Yea, theirs is a happy, fulfilling path. Aum.

SUTRA 27

All my followers are generous to a fault, tithing and giving creatively without thought of reward. All have cultivated an unshakeable faith, believing firmly in God, Gods, guru and our path to enlightenment. Aum.

SUTRA 28

All my followers are madly devout in their worship, and cultivate divine love through daily ritual and deep meditation. All eagerly hear the scriptures, study the teachings and listen to the wise of our lineage. Aum.

SUTRA 29

All my followers shall cultivate the powers of cognition, developing a spiritual will and intellect with their Satguru's guidance. They take religious vows, rules and observances and never waver in fulfilling them. Aum.

SUTRA 30

All followers shall chant their holy mantra daily, counting each recitation on the sacred rudraksha beads. All shall practice some form of austerity, performing regular disciplines, penance and sacrifice. Aum Namasivaya.

Ahimsa, the Foremost Discipline

SUTRA 31

None of my followers shall intentionally kill or injure any person, nor harm anyone in any way. Nonviolence, physically, mentally and emotionally, is their highest ethical code. Yea, theirs is a kindly and holy life. Aum.

SUTRA 32

None of my followers shall intentionally kill or injure any creature whatsoever. Full of compassion, free of the instinct to kill, they are never a source of fear, pain or hurtfulness. They perceive their oneness with all. Aum.

SUTRA 33

My followers are forbidden to escape life's experience through suicide. However, in cases of terminal illness, under strict community regulation, tradition does allow fasting as a means of *mors voluntaria religiosa.* Aum.

SUTRA 34

None of my followers should ever speak of, listen to or look at portrayals of pornography or excessive violence. Nor should they ever humiliate themselves or others, even under the pretext of telling the truth. Aum.

SUTRA 35

All my followers must speak only that which is true, kind, helpful and necessary. They never use profane language, bear false witness against another, engage in slander or backbiting or even listen to such talk. Aum Namasivaya.

Regrettable Exceptions to Ahimsa

SUTRA 36

For followers unable to fulfill ahimsa perfectly I begrudgingly recognize three exceptions which preserve one life over another. These must be applied sparingly, after every noninjurious alternative has been tried. Aum.

SUTRA 37

My followers may, in the face of danger, elect to injure or kill to protect their own life or that of another, or to defend the community as a soldier or as a civic servant in the line of duty. This is the first exception. Aum.

SUTRA 38

My followers may elect to preserve the life and health of a person or creature under their care by forfeiting the life of lesser creatures, such as worms or microbes, that pose a threat. This is the second exception. Aum.

SUTRA 39

My followers may elect to protect the home, the village and the nation by eradicating predators, pests, bacteria and disease-carrying creatures that threaten their health or safety. This is the third and final exception. Aum.

SUTRA 40

All my followers shall adopt the principle to not kill even household pests, but to stop their entry, to not kill garden insects or predators, but keep them away by natural means. This is the highest ideal. Aum Namasivaya.

Reverence for the Environment

SUTRA 41

My followers shall be stewards of trees and plants, fish and birds, bees and reptiles, animals and creatures of every shape and kind, and become the trusted friends of humans of every caste, creed, color and sex. Aum.

SUTRA 42

All my followers are interracial, international citizens of the earth, thinking globally and acting locally. They are defenders of all human cultures, languages and peoples, never offending one to promote another. Aum.

SUTRA 43

All my followers shall honor and revere the world around them as God's creation and work for the protection of the earth's diversity and resources to achieve the goal of a secure and lasting environment. Aum.

SUTRA 44

My followers should not acquire or condone the use of endangered plants or animals, or products from exploited species, such as furs, ivory, reptile skin, tortoise shell, or items produced using cruel animal testing. Aum.

SUTRA 45

All my followers must be frugal and resourceful, avoiding waste and being conservative with nature's precious resources. They store a three-to-twelve-month supply of food according to their means. Aum Namasivaya.

Self-Control

SUTRA 46

All followers shall observe the eightfold celibacy toward everyone but their spouse, renouncing sexual fantasy, glorification, flirtation, lustful glances, secret love talk, amorous longing, rendezvous and intercourse. Aum.

SUTRA 47

It is well known that all my followers can absorb any amount of praise. But those who can withstand mental, emotional persecution, even physical torment, with the same infinite capacity are indeed my followers. Aum.

SUTRA 48

All my followers should surround themselves with traditional images, music and song each day. Never, never do they listen to the crude music of the lower world, which teaches the antithesis of the path of light. Aum.

SUTRA 49

Followers may watch television, for recreation and to keep informed about the world's contemporary ways. Viewing should not exceed two hours a day. Nudity, vulgarity and excessive violence are to be avoided. Aum.

SUTRA 50

My followers realize adversity is a boon from the Gods, an accumulation of karmas to be faced head-on, without cringing. They have already earned the strength to handle courageously all that comes. Aum Namasivaya.

Regarding Worldly Activities

SUTRA 51

My followers shall not indulge or engage professionally in gambling, lotteries or games of chance, even through others. Gambling erodes the social fabric, assuring the certain loss of many for the hopeful gain of a few. Aum.

SUTRA 52

All my followers know bad money can never do good deeds and refuse soiled funds from any source. Nor can good money used wrongly reap right results. Ill-gotten money is never well-spent, but has a curse upon it. Aum.

SUTRA 53

None of my followers should ever accept bribes from anyone, nor offer bribes to another, no matter how seemingly necessary or culturally accepted this practice may be. Jai, they fight for the mercy of honesty. Aum.

SUTRA 54

All my followers treasure humility. They never boast or sit in prideful postures—with one foot placed on the thigh, or with arms folded or chin held exceedingly high. They never point with their index finger. Aum.

SUTRA 55

None of my followers should associate with thieves, addicts, atheists or those inclined to sexual promiscuity, nor those who feign devotion, are ungrateful, selfish, vicious or possess many impurities. Aum Namasivaya.

Part Two

Belief

Authorized Scriptures

SUTRA 56

My followers shall recognize that the primary scriptural authority of our lineage derives from the Saiva Agamas and the four noble Vedas, which include the Upanishads. Ours is a Vedic-Agamic tradition. Aum.

SUTRA 57

All followers shall revere as sacred scripture *The Holy Bible of the Saivite Hindu Religion*—which includes Rishi Tirumular's *Tirumantiram* and Saint Tiruvalluvar's *Tirukural*—and not act against its advice. Aum.

SUTRA 58

Followers shall revere as sacred scripture the profound hymns of the Tamil Saivite saints—most especially Sambandar, Appar, Sundarar, Manikkavasagar and Thayumanavar—and the Natha *Yoga Sutras* of Patanjali. Aum.

SUTRA 59

All my followers shall revere as sacred scripture the songs of Sage Yogaswami, called *Natchintanai*, which entirely embody the teachings of our lineage and command one and all to "Know thy Self by thy self." Aum.

SUTRA 60

All my followers shall hold as sacred scripture the *Hindu Catechism and Creed, The Lord Subramaniam Shastras* and all my other sacred texts and discourses, including these *Nandinatha Sutras*. Aum Namasivaya.

The Nature of God

SUTRA 61

All my followers shall take pride in the fact that the philosophical basis of the fellowship lies in the unity of Siddhanta and Vedanta. This mysterious dance of dualism and nondualism is called monistic theism. Aum.

SUTRA 62

Followers shall continuously study, live and enthusiastically preach to the peoples of the world our theological doctrine, called by various names: monistic theism, Advaita Siddhanta and Suddha Saiva Siddhanta. Aum.

SUTRA 63

My followers all believe that Lord Siva is God, whose Absolute Being, Parasivam, transcends time, form and space. The yogi silently exclaims, "It is not this. It is not that." Yea, such an inscrutable God is God Siva. Aum.

SUTRA 64

My followers all believe that Lord Siva is God, whose immanent nature of love is the substratum or Primal Substance and Pure Consciousness flowing through all form. It is pure existence, knowledge and bliss. Aum.

SUTRA 65

My followers all believe that Lord Siva is God, whose immanent nature is the Primal Soul, Supreme Mahadeva, Siva-Sakti, the Creator, Preserver and Destroyer of all that exists. He is Lord of lords. Aum Namasivaya.

The Nature of Souls and World

SUTRA 66

My followers all believe that each soul is created by Lord Siva and is identical to Him, and that this identity will be fully realized by all souls when the bondage of anava, karma and maya is removed by His Grace. Aum.

SUTRA 67

My followers all believe in three worlds: the gross plane, where souls take on physical bodies; the subtle plane, where souls take on astral bodies; and the causal plane, where souls exist in their self-effulgent form. Aum.

SUTRA 68

My followers all believe that religion is the harmonious working together of the three worlds and that this harmony can be created through temple worship, wherein the beings of all three worlds can communicate. Aum.

SUTRA 69

My followers all believe in the Mahadeva Lord Ganesha, Son of Siva-Sakti, to whom they must first supplicate before beginning any worship or task. His rule is compassionate. His law is just. Justice is His mind. Aum.

SUTRA 70

My followers all believe in the Mahadeva Lord Muruga, Son of Siva-Sakti, whose Vel of Grace dissolves the bondages of ignorance. The yogi, locked in lotus, venerates Muruga. His mind becomes calm. Aum Namasivaya.

Karma, Evil and Wisdom

SUTRA 71

My followers all believe in the law of karma—that one must reap the effects of all actions he has caused—and that each soul continues to reincarnate until all karmas are resolved and Moksha, Liberation, is attained. Aum.

SUTRA 72

My followers all believe that the performance of virtuous living, temple worship and yoga, leading to Parasivam through the grace of the living Satguru, is absolutely necessary to bring forth the wisdom state. Aum.

SUTRA 73

My followers all hold as their affirmation of faith *Anbe Sivamayam Satyame Parasivam*—"God Siva is immanent love and transcendent reality." This is a perfect summary of Saiva Siddhanta's exquisite truth. Aum.

SUTRA 74

Followers all believe in the Panchakshara Mantra, the five sacred syllables "Namasivaya," as Saivism's foremost and essential mantra. The secret of Namasivaya is to hear it from the right lips at the right time. Aum.

SUTRA 75

My followers all believe that there is no intrinsic evil. Evil has no source, unless the source of evil's seeming be ignorance itself. Yea, they are truly compassionate, knowing there is no intrinsic evil. Aum Namasivaya.

Part Three

Practice

Temple Worship

SUTRA 76

Followers shall absolutely have a fantastically awesome home shrine dedicated solely for worship of Tiruvadi, Siva Lingam, Nataraja, Ardhanarisvara, Muruga and Ganesha. This is the home's most beautiful room. Aum.

SUTRA 77

All my followers may perform the Saiva atmartha puja, but only in home shrines and fellowship missions. Unless formally, traditionally authorized, they are forbidden to learn, teach or perform the parartha puja. Aum.

SUTRA 78

My followers should settle in areas where Ganesha, Muruga or Siva temples exist for their frequent pilgrimage, worship and spiritual security. None should live farther than a day's journey from such sacred sanctuaries. Aum.

SUTRA 79

My followers shall hold as most sacred and pilgrimage to each at least once: Siva's Iraivan Temple on Kauai, His Himalayan and Gangetic abodes, His five elemental temples and the Madurai Meenakshi citadel. Aum.

SUTRA 80

My followers shall deeply revere and pilgrimage to Lord Muruga's six great temples, Lord Ganesha's many temples and roadside shrines, especially Kumbalavalai, and the holy sepulchers of our lineage. Aum Namasivaya.

Cultural Accomplishments

SUTRA 81

All followers shall learn a skill or craft requiring the use of the hands, such as pottery, sewing, knitting, weaving, painting, gardening, baking or the building arts, to manifest creative benefits for family and community. Aum.

SUTRA 82

All my followers should perfect a cultural accomplishment, be it a form of art, singing, drama, dance or a musical instrument of Lord Siva's ensemble (veena, mridangam, tambura, cymbals and bamboo flute). Aum.

SUTRA 83

All my followers should embrace Sanskrit as their language of ritual worship, Shum as their language of meditation, and Tyaf as their script for offering prayers to the Gods and devas through the sacred fire. Aum.

SUTRA 84

All followers shall use the Indian lunar calendar as a daily guide to auspicious planning, especially for travel, innovation, ceremonial rites and other major life events. Our year begins with the Vedic month of Aries. Aum.

SUTRA 85

All followers must embrace and master the gestures, attitudes, customs, ways of worship, dress and refinements of Asian Hindu protocol. They learn by living and studying with traditional Saivites. Aum Namasivaya.

Spiritual Study

SUTRA 86

All my followers shall explore *The Master Course* as their lifetime study, allowing its mystical and practical teachings to light their inner path. In these profound lessons they discover the meaning of life's many lessons. Aum.

SUTRA 87

Followers study the five states of mind: conscious, subconscious, sub-subconscious, subsuperconscious and superconscious. They let go of negative attachments and become master of mind, body and emotions. Aum.

SUTRA 88

Followers know that to succeed on the path they must change their subconscious by remolding its magnetic forces with new ideas and concepts. It is through the power of affirmation that this is accomplished. Aum.

SUTRA 89

All followers learn and perfect the five steps to enlightenment: attention, concentration, meditation, contemplation and finally samadhi, wherein they realize the unspeakable Truth, known only by the knower. Aum.

SUTRA 90

My followers study these three to discover the mysteries of being: the subtle bodies of man, the aura, which is a rainbow of thought and feeling, and the fourteen chakras or centers of consciousness. Aum Namasivaya.

Occultism

SUTRA 91

My followers shall not involve themselves in trances, astral projection, past-and-future-life readings or psychic mentors. Nor do they consult astrologers or palmists other than those approved by the preceptor. Aum.

SUTRA 92

My followers may spontaneously experience but must not practice clairvoyance, clairaudience, astral projection, lucid dreaming, trance mediumship, mind-reading, fortunetelling, magic or other occult arts. Aum.

SUTRA 93

All followers are under the Satguru's psychic protection and remain untouched by negative occult forces. Those who are yet prone to such afflictions, however, should seek relief according to the advice of his achariyas. Aum.

SUTRA 94

None of my followers should indulge in remembrance or interpretation of dreams unless as a special discipline from their guru. They intentionally forget dreams and positively concern themselves with waking life. Aum.

SUTRA 95

My followers shall practice the ancient tradition of burning prayers to the devas and Mahadevas through the sacred fire, but only within fellowship missions or other shrines designated by the preceptor. Aum Namasivaya.

Spiritual Disciplines

SUTRA 96

My followers shall daily arise two hours before sunrise, bathe, don fresh clothing, apply holy ash and sit in a clean, quiet place for religious disciplines. On weekends and vacations, or when ill, they may arise later. Aum.

SUTRA 97

All my followers shall worship ritually each day facing east or north, chant the guru mantra, recite 108 repetitions of their mantra and remain in scriptural study, meditation and yoga until the dim light of dawn. Aum.

SUTRA 98

All followers practice the basic yogas—bhakti, karma and hatha, as I have outlined them—throughout life, and more as life goes on. They know self-mastery yokes the fire within with That which quells the fire. Aum.

SUTRA 99

My followers who qualify may practice the advanced yogas—japa, raja and kundalini—but only under adept guidance, realizing that, unless firmly harnessed, the kundalini can manifest uncontrollable desires. Aum.

SUTRA 100

All followers who are victim to anger, jealousy or hatred should not meditate or perform japa. They must perform bhakti and karma yoga to raise consciousness before proceeding deeply within. Aum Namasivaya.

Personal Disciplines

SUTRA 101

All followers shall, before preparing any meal, place in a vessel one handful of uncooked rice. This modest sharing is offered at the Satguru's Tiruvadi each full-moon day to be shared by him with the less fortunate. Aum.

SUTRA 102

All my followers keep a special coffer in their shrine into which they place a few coins each day for Iraivan Temple. They bring or send this fund to Kauai Aadheenam each year during the Maha Sivaratri festival. Aum.

SUTRA 103

Followers so inclined may perform kavadi during Muruga festivals where custom allows. They may also lie on beds of nails, walk on fire and undertake other forms of penance to build character and atone for sins. Aum.

SUTRA 104

All followers must keep their home environment clean and uncluttered to create a strong spiritual vibration and not attract negative forces. They seek fresh air and sunshine and surround themselves with beauty. Aum.

SUTRA 105

My followers should sleep with the head placed south or east, after chanting and meditating to prepare for a great journey to the inner worlds. If awakened, they sit up and meditate before returning to sleep. Aum Namasivaya.

Symbols, Mantras and Names

SUTRA 106

All my followers, men and women, boys and girls, shall wear a rudraksha bead around the neck at all times, and holy ash and the proper mark on the forehead for religious functions, and in public when appropriate. Aum.

SUTRA 107

My followers observe the custom of saying "Om Namasivaya" or "Om Sivaya" when greeting others and when parting. The more general greetings "vanakkam," "namaste" and "namaskaram" are also permissible. Aum.

SUTRA 108

Just before sleep, all my followers utter: "Anbe Sivamayam Satyame Parasivam," while pondering the great depths of this affirmation. Upon awakening, their first words are "Anbe Sivamayam Satyame Parasivam." Aum.

SUTRA 109

My followers chant the bhojana mantra before each meal, offering thankful praise to God, Gods and guru. They chant the shanti mantra to begin and end all meetings, invoking peace and one-mindedness. Aum.

SUTRA 110

All my followers shall bear and legally register their Saivite Hindu name, first and last, and use it proudly each day in all circumstances, never concealing or altering it to adjust to non-Hindu cultures. Aum Namasivaya.

Part Four

Personal Life

Diet and Food

SUTRA 111

All my followers shall cook and eat in the balanced, varied, time-tested, Indian ayurvedic manner. They take food with their fingers to energize it. One day a week, they may enjoy cuisine from other world cultures. Aum.

SUTRA 112

My followers avoid junk food. They eat freshly cooked foods and drink unchilled water plentifully and with meals. At least at the main meal, all six tastes (sweet, salty, sour, pungent, bitter and astringent) are served. Aum.

SUTRA 113

All my followers should adhere to the ayurvedic principles of eating at regular times, only when hungry, always seated, at a moderate pace, never between meals, in a disturbed atmosphere or when emotionally upset. Aum.

SUTRA 114

All my followers eat in moderation at each meal. The first portion should not exceed what can be held in two hands cupped together. If still hungry, one more handful may be taken. Eating right is good medicine. Aum.

SUTRA 115

All my followers should fast on water, herb teas or fruit juices for one day each week or month, on Friday or the thirteenth day of the dark fortnight. However, they shall avoid prolonged, ascetic fasting. Aum Namasivaya.

Health and Exercise

SUTRA 116

All my followers shall eat a strictly vegetarian diet. They understand that higher consciousness depends on the chemistry of foods consumed and thus forbid themselves to eat meat, fish, shellfish, fowl or eggs. Aum.

SUTRA 117

My followers know that wellness is balance. If the imbalance called illness occurs, they first apply self-healing, then turn to an ayurvedic doctor. In emergencies, they seek aid from an appropriate medical practitioner. Aum.

SUTRA 118

My followers know the truest healing powers reside in the mind, at the quantum level. They embrace ayurveda, but may also use other proven healing arts, such as allopathy, naturopathy, acupuncture and chiropractic. Aum.

SUTRA 119

My followers must not involve their minds in inordinate physical worry nor indulge in personal health studies other than ayurveda. Nor should they adopt diverse diets unless undergoing medical treatment. Aum.

SUTRA 120

My followers shall keep strong and healthy, exercising moderately for one-half hour each day through such activities as brisk walking, swimming, salutations to the sun, hatha yoga and vigorous work. Aum Namasivaya.

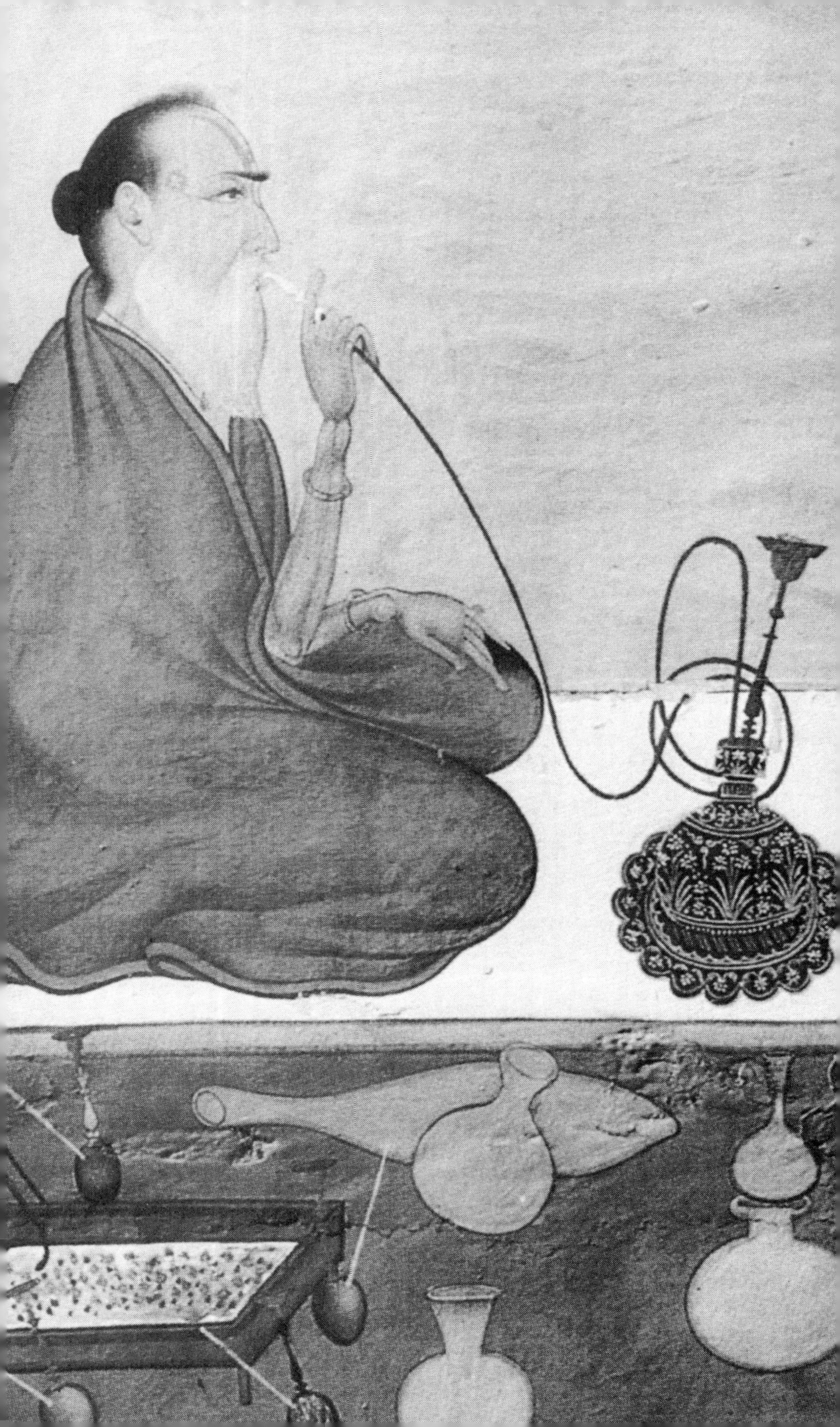

Tobacco and Drugs

SUTRA 121

My followers shall not smoke or chew tobacco or inhale snuff. They know the addictive power of nicotine and value their health and longevity as of primary importance to fulfill karmas and serve their community. Aum.

SUTRA 122

All my followers are forbidden to use amphetamines, barbiturates, cocaine, heroin, psychedelics and all mind-altering concoctions not prescribed by a licensed physician. They know the destabilizing effects. Aum.

SUTRA 123

My followers must educate their children to refuse, by saying "no," any and all known or unknown drugs offered to them by friends or strangers. Well-informed by caring parents, children avoid these dangers. Aum.

SUTRA 124

My followers know that dangerous drugs awaken simultaneously the chakra of divine love and those of fear, confusion and malice, producing vast mood swings and a stunted intellect. They dread this chemical chaos. Aum.

SUTRA 125

My followers stand against drugs and never mix with those who use them nor listen to talk extolling them. The drug culture and its demonic music erode the fabric of human character and culture. Aum Namasivaya.

Guidelines Regarding Alcohol

SUTRA 126

All strong and intoxicating distilled alcohols are forbidden to my followers. They may moderately partake of the family of wines and beers, including honey mead. These are wholesome when properly enjoyed. Aum.

SUTRA 127

Even in moderation, my followers are forbidden to drink alcohol in solitude, when depressed or under extreme stress. When one is emotionally unstable, alcohol inhibits the ability to confront and solve problems. Aum.

SUTRA 128

When necessary, my followers should gently enforce temperance among peers by providing joyous nonalcoholic alternatives. They know that those unable to maintain moderation may have to abstain entirely. Aum.

SUTRA 129

My women followers are forbidden by customs of decorum and demureness to drink alcohol in public. During pregnancy, they abstain completely to protect the health and well-being of their unborn child. Aum.

SUTRA 130

Followers know that should alcohol become a spiritual obstacle or a burden to their family or the fellowship, despite the help of peers or elders, it is the preceptor's duty to deny the privilege altogether. Aum Namasivaya.

The Four Stages of Life

SUTRA 131

My followers shall honor and conscientiously fulfill the duties of each of life's four progressive stages of dharma: student (age 12–24), householder (25–48), respected elder (49–72) and religious solitaire after age 72. Aum.

SUTRA 132

All my followers recognize that the natural human life span is 120 years. They should confidently plan ahead at each 40-year juncture. Elders shall counsel, as needed, persons in life transitions, around 40 and 80. Aum.

SUTRA 133

All my followers should grow old gracefully, without fear, knowing that the soul is immortal and the mental body does not age, but becomes stronger and more mature, as do the emotions if regulated stage by stage. Aum.

SUTRA 134

My followers must intensify their religious disciplines after retirement, give guidance to the younger generations, teach, encourage and uplift, manage orphanages and create endowments to educate the young. Aum.

SUTRA 135

Male followers may renounce the world after age 72. As unordained, self-declared sannyasins, they must sever all ties with the fellowship and live as homeless mendicants among the monks of India. Aum Namasivaya.

Approaching Death

SUTRA 136

My followers shall provide spiritual counseling to the terminally ill, blessed with the knowledge of impending death, showing ways to resolve the past so that Siva consciousness is their bridge during transition. Aum.

SUTRA 137

My followers preparing for death must mend fences, execute reconciliations, make friends of enemies and seek forgivenesses before their transition, lest unresolved karmas go to seed, to bear fruit in future births. Aum.

SUTRA 138

All my followers who are dying must concentrate on their mantra and find solace in our holy teachings of the soul's immortality, ever seeking the highest realizations as they consciously, joyously release the world. Aum.

SUTRA 139

My followers should be at home among family rather than in a hospital during the last days of their life. They should avoid the artificial extension of life. As death approaches, a loved one must keep a prayerful vigil. Aum.

SUTRA 140

All my followers should at the moment of death depart the body through the crown chakra and enter consciously into the clear white light and beyond. A perfect transition surely leads to Liberation. Aum Namasivaya.

About Death's Aftermath

SUTRA 141

My followers shall cremate their dead. Burial is forbidden. No embalming should be permitted, and no autopsy unless required by law. Ashes should be ceremoniously offered into a sacred river or an ocean. Aum.

SUTRA 142

My followers shall arrange swift cremation of the departed, within twenty-four hours. This purifies the physical elements and releases the deceased into the causal plane where souls exist in their self-effulgent form. Aum.

SUTRA 143

At the death of a follower, family and friends gather for funeral rites in the home. They prepare the body and arrange for the cremation. On the seventh day, a photo is honored and food is offered to the deceased. Aum.

SUTRA 144

Family and friends of a deceased follower hold memorial rites on the thirty-first day, cleaning the home and making offerings of food to ancestors and the departed. This is repeated one year from the day of death. Aum.

SUTRA 145

Knowing that the soul is deathless, my followers must never suffer undue or prolonged sorrow for the departed, lest they bind these souls to earth. They rejoice in the continuing journey of loved ones. Aum Namasivaya.

Part Five

Livelihood

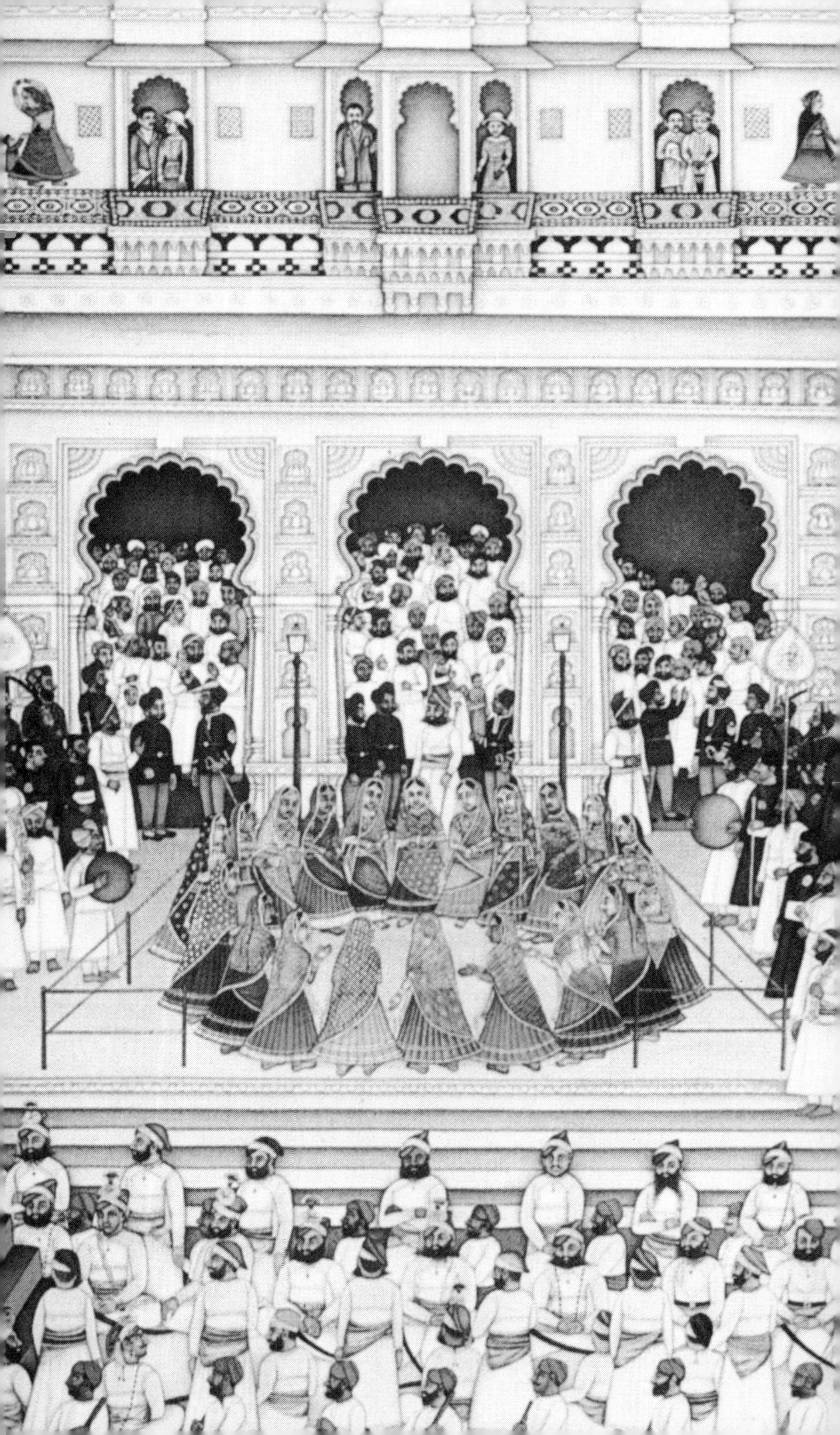

About Wealth

SUTRA 146

My followers remain dignified in deprivation and humble in prosperity. They know one can be spiritually rich in poverty and spiritually impoverished in affluence and choose to live bountifully in both worlds. Aum.

SUTRA 147

My householder followers should own their home and save for their retirement. They must live within their means, in dwellings suitable to their wealth, and be regular and completely honest in paying their taxes. Aum.

SUTRA 148

All my followers must keep a monthly budget and regulate their expenses according to their revenues. They should never indulge in extravagant buying, for to spend in excess of one's income is to invite misery. Aum.

SUTRA 149

My followers must keep a regular monthly and yearly accounting of income and expenses, and accurate records of all transactions. In every business deal, they will assure that all parties are benefitted and content. Aum.

SUTRA 150

All my followers shall dutifully prepare a formal, written final will and testament, even when they are young, which abundantly provides for their family, their religion, their lineage and the fellowship. Aum Namasivaya.

God's Money

SUTRA 151

All my followers shall take a tithing vow and joyously give ten percent of their income to the lineage each month. This is Siva's money. To use it otherwise is a sin that will reap loss in excess of all anticipated gain. Aum.

SUTRA 152

All my followers shall consider tithing their first expense. Twice each year, of their own volition, they provide a written reconciliation, including with it all unremitted tithing to bring themselves current. Aum.

SUTRA 153

All my followers know the spiritual law that by tithing freely and joyously, with the consciousness of plenty, they become receptive to God's blessings and draw to themselves abundance and happy experiences. Aum.

SUTRA 154

All my followers of means must utilize their wealth and resources to strengthen the mission of the lineage, to support temples, publish books, establish endowments and scholarships and perform elaborate rituals. Aum.

SUTRA 155

My followers should observe the tradition of expressing appreciation to their Satguru in the form of an annual love-offering during Guru Purnima in July-August, enabling him to help others on the path. Aum Namasivaya.

Politics and Vocation

SUTRA 156

All my followers shall be patriotic to their nation and loyal to community, family and environment. They strive to give to, advance, support and defend their community. They are never predators living upon it. Aum.

SUTRA 157

All my followers who qualify may with vigor and indomitable will enter the political arena, conquer opposition and rise to the top to shower good fortune, justice, peace, tranquility and care on all peoples. Aum.

SUTRA 158

All my followers are free to pursue the politics of their choice. However, they shall not subscribe to doctrines that advocate revolution or deny religion, nor organize among other followers for any political purpose. Aum.

SUTRA 159

My followers should choose professions that are helpful and beneficial to all, never destructive, divisive or exploitative. Yea, they are ministers of the divine, missionaries of a future tranquility yet to be developed. Aum.

SUTRA 160

In the event of famine, invasion, tyranny or such extreme conditions that threaten wealth or life, followers should migrate to a place free of harassment where their spiritual life can continue unhindered. Aum Namasivaya.

Instructions for Parliamentarians

SUTRA 161

All my followers who are parliamentarians shall live fully in conformity with the sacred scriptures, extend full protection to their people as they would their own children and never bend to graft or corruption. Aum.

SUTRA 162

My followers who are parliamentarians must take pains to spread religious tenets and tolerant human values among their constituents. They must commission competent people to enhance all the great world faiths. Aum.

SUTRA 163

My followers who are parliamentarians should have as their platform justice for all and enmity toward none. They know that to show favoritism toward one group over another sows the seeds of their own downfall. Aum.

SUTRA 164

All my followers who are parliamentarians shall face and work through each challenge that comes and never be forced to abdicate. They maintain their post as long as possible, then seek the next highest position. Aum.

SUTRA 165

My followers who are parliamentarians shall give equal boons to every spiritual sect under their jurisdiction as if it were their own. They know a society is only as free as the freedoms given its minorities. Aum Namasivaya.

Instructions for Scientists

SUTRA 166

My followers who are scientists shall be protectors of humanity and stewards of the earth. They must never compromise their ethics for financial rewards nor release inventions before proven safe and beneficial. Aum.

SUTRA 167

My followers who are scientifically and alchemistically inclined should approach each investigation in awe, consider themselves servants of the divine and subjugate themselves to the guidance of their preceptor. Aum.

SUTRA 168

My followers who are scientists or medical researchers shall not participate in product testing that is harmful to the subject. They are forbidden to join in any enterprise that promotes either death or destruction. Aum.

SUTRA 169

My scientist followers should concentrate their energies on bettering the world, conserving its goods and enabling humans to live in greater harmony with nature and one another. They are examples to mankind. Aum.

SUTRA 170

All my followers who are scientists must remember that secret is always sacred and resist the urge to share everything they discover. Knowledge can be dangerous in the hands of the unscrupulous. Aum Namasivaya.

Part Six

Men and Women

Instructions for Men

SUTRA 171

Each of my men followers shall speak to and associate with men. Conversations with women, especially the wives of other men, should not be prolonged, and then directing his gaze at the hairline, not into the eyes. Aum.

SUTRA 172

All my male followers go out of their way to express respect, bordering on reverence, for women. Thus, they forbid themselves to watch vulgar shows or to maintain relations with lustful or promiscuous women. Aum.

SUTRA 173

My male followers should never enter into argument with women, nor antagonize or tease them in any way. They must always be protective, helpful and understanding, thus honoring the mother spirit within them. Aum.

SUTRA 174

All my male followers must whenever possible dress in impeccable, traditional Hindu attire, especially when attending religious and cultural events. Yea, their outer elegance is only equaled by their inner dignity. Aum.

SUTRA 175

My male followers should, on arriving home from work, immediately bathe and enter their shrine for the blessings of Gods and guru to dispel worldly forces and regain the state of Siva consciousness. Aum Namasivaya.

Instructions for Husbands

SUTRA 176

Each of my married male followers shall love and care for his wife, even if she is blind, ailing or poor, uneducated or uninterested in his occupation. He shall never strike, speak harshly to her or ignore her needs. Aum.

SUTRA 177

Followers who are husbands should not develop long-term associations with young, beautiful women, even in their professional life. Nor should they associate with widows or divorcees not closely related to them. Aum.

SUTRA 178

When away from home, all my followers who are husbands should contact their wife each day to express their love and inquire about her day. They avoid rowdy company and never visit another woman's home. Aum.

SUTRA 179

Each follower who is a husband must spend time with his wife and children daily. Monday, Siva's day, is family home evening, and at least one night a month is devoted to the wife alone in an activity of her choice. Aum.

SUTRA 180

My followers who are husbands should spend equitably among all family members. They never utilize the family income to indulge their own desires while neglecting the needs or interests of others. Aum Namasivaya.

Instructions for Women

SUTRA 181

My women followers shall dress impeccably, in traditional, rich Hindu costumes with jewelry, especially for religious and cultural events. They never expose breasts, navel or thighs. Yea, they are outrageously elegant. Aum.

SUTRA 182

My women followers never become angry with a man, maliciously accuse or verbally beat him, nor employ other emotional controls, such as disdain, accusation, crying, prolonged pouting or extended silence. Aum.

SUTRA 183

My women followers should speak to and associate with women. Conversations with males, especially married men, should not be excessive. Any intimate exchange of energies is avoided by looking at the hairline. Aum.

SUTRA 184

Women followers shall be allowed to rest and renew regenerative forces during their monthly menses, refraining from heavy or demanding work. They do not enter temples or home shrines or approach holy men. Aum.

SUTRA 185

My followers who are women shall consider it their special responsibility to protect, preserve and promote the Saiva Dharma by living its culture and systematically passing on its tenets to the children. Aum Namasivaya.

Instructions for Wives

SUTRA 186

Each of my married women followers shall worship her wedding pendant each morning. It betokens her dear husband—whom she reveres as Siva Himself—and the spiritual bond and goals that she shares with him. Aum.

SUTRA 187

Each of my married women followers shall observe the tradition of arising before her husband, to bathe, ready the shrine and prepare his morning beverage. First up and last to retire, she is in charge of her home. Aum.

SUTRA 188

Each of my married women followers shall at mealtimes observe the ancient tradition of serving her husband and family first. When they are satisfied, she is fulfilled and only then sits down for her own meal. Aum.

SUTRA 189

Each married women follower must love and serve her husband, even if he is blind or ailing, lazy, poor or uninterested in worship and service to God, and under no circumstances criticize or speak harshly to him. Aum.

SUTRA 190

None of my followers who are wives should develop long-term associations with young, handsome men, even in professional life, nor associate with widowers or divorcés not closely related to them. Aum Namasivaya.

Instructions for the Widowed

SUTRA 191

All my followers who are widows or widowers shall serve God faithfully. If they elect to remarry, it must be a spiritual union, astrologically compatible and blessed by the Satguru and their religious community. Aum.

SUTRA 192

All my widowed followers who do not remarry must practice strict continence. They dedicate their lives to God and transmute sexual forces into the higher chakras by heeding the traditional rules of celibacy. Aum.

SUTRA 193

My widowed followers who elect not to remarry should wear unprovocative white clothing, never yellow or orange, as renunciates do. Widows wear no cosmetics, marriage pendant, flowers or elaborate jewelry. Aum.

SUTRA 194

My followers who are widows or widowers should throw themselves into their yoga practices. Though their loss is great, so too is their opportunity for religious service and the attainment of the highest spiritual goals. Aum.

SUTRA 195

Widowed followers not intending to remarry may wear the single rudraksha bead and holy ash, but their forehead dot is sandalpaste, not red powder. They do not participate in family rites of passage. Aum Namasivaya.

Instructions for the Single

SUTRA 196

All my young followers shall take the celibacy vow and remain virgin until marriage. For lasting happiness and mutual spiritual purpose, fellowship members marry another member chosen by parents and Satguru. Aum.

SUTRA 197

All unmarried adolescent and adult followers are considered brahmacharis or brahmacharinis, bound to the traditions of chastity that our fellowship prescribes, whether they have taken a celibacy vow or not. Aum.

SUTRA 198

My female followers electing not to marry may live the brahmacharini's celibate life, keeping simple vows and always wearing white. By this the world knows they are unavailable, having chosen the path of devotion. Aum.

SUTRA 199

Male followers choosing not to marry take up the celibate life, keeping simple vows and wearing white. To be a swami candidate, they must begin the twelve-year period of monastic training prior to age twenty-five. Aum.

SUTRA 200

All male followers inclined to throw down the world and enter the monastery should read and take to heart my *Holy Orders of Sannyas* and adjust themselves to its ideals before requesting training. Aum Namasivaya.

Part Seven

The Family

Hospitality

SUTRA 201

Hospitality should flow from my followers like sweet music from a veena. Guests are treated as God. Friends, acquaintances and even strangers are humbled by the overwhelming, ever-flowing attention received. Aum.

SUTRA 202

My followers must serve holy men and ascetics of all sects, with food, money and clothes, according to their means. They happily care for these living archives of dharma and never quarrel or debate with them. Aum.

SUTRA 203

My followers who are householders are urged to visit one another's homes and grow together in Godliness. Some religious ceremony or service shall always be a part of their gathering. Yea, they are a one family. Aum.

SUTRA 204

My followers should venerate the aged for their knowledge, their guidance, their wisdom, their compassion and their existence. Followers, no matter what their age, must never disrespect those older than they. Aum.

SUTRA 205

My followers see that the spirit of helping and taking care of one another prevails between family and family, and monastery and family. The group helps the individual and the individual helps the group. Aum Namasivaya.

Household Ethics

SUTRA 206

Each of my married men followers shall strive to fulfill male dharma, assuring the future of society and the family through protecting his dear wife and children and providing abundantly for their every need. Aum.

SUTRA 207

Each of my married women followers shall strive to fulfill female dharma, perpetuating the race, family and the faith through remaining in the home to nurture, guide and strengthen her husband and children. Aum.

SUTRA 208

My followers know the most stable societies are based on the extended family. They may merge individuals with families and families with families in a one home, for economy, sharing and enhanced spirituality. Aum.

SUTRA 209

All my followers who are householders shall serve their parents and close relatives all through life. The elderly especially should be comforted, adulated at auspicious times and never left alone for extended periods. Aum.

SUTRA 210

My householder followers do not have adult guests in their home for more than three nights unless related by blood or marriage. Thus they protect family sanctity and avoid magnetic entanglements. Aum Namasivaya.

Raising Children

SUTRA 211

My followers consider the raising of children a sacred responsibility. Based on astrology, tradition and wise counsel, they shall formulate patterns that cultivate each child's inherent talents and higher nature. Aum.

SUTRA 212

My followers who are parents should creatively train their boys in technical skills, girls in the arts of home-making, and both in the basic accomplishments of music, art, sewing, cooking and home management. Aum.

SUTRA 213

All my followers who are parents love their offspring and shall govern them with kindness. They are forbidden to spank, slap or hit their children, use harsh or angry words, neglect or abuse them in any way. Aum.

SUTRA 214

My followers are forbidden to govern their offspring through fear. If they do, elders must counsel the parents and console the children. Parents who fail to correct their attitudes and actions must be ostracized. Aum.

SUTRA 215

My followers must provide their children the essential sacraments at the proper times, especially name-giving, first feeding, head-shaving, ear-piercing, first learning, rites of puberty, and marriage. Aum Namasivaya.

Preserving Family Unity

SUTRA 216

All my followers who are parents shall direct children through positive affirmations, never with questions such as, "Why don't you begin your homework?" lest they encourage insecurity, disobedience and rebellion. Aum.

SUTRA 217

All my followers who are parents shall preserve family unity by not granting children financial independence. When money is given, all expenditures are approved by parents, and change is returned with accounting. Aum.

SUTRA 218

Followers should not allow children, before college, to hold any job, even during vacations, lest money desires distract them from education. This does not apply to the family business, which they help without pay. Aum.

SUTRA 219

My followers shall require unmarried sons or daughters living with them, having finished school and begun a career, to submit their earnings to the family fund. Allowance received must be accounted for in full. Aum.

SUTRA 220

My followers who are parents must set good standards and provide needed guidance by making all major decisions for offspring living within their home, even after they are educated and independent. Aum Namasivaya.

Preparing Youth for Adult Life

SUTRA 221

My followers shall abide by the traditional wisdom of bringing sons and daughters into the skills, profession or business of the family at a young age. This is family dharma, family bonding, family perpetuation. Aum.

SUTRA 222

My followers must teach their sons and daughters, between ages four and ten, about the cycles of life and the principles of virtue, and when puberty arrives, require them to take the vow of celibacy until marriage. Aum.

SUTRA 223

My young followers shall be taught to protect their chastity as a treasure and to save all acts of sexual intimacy for their future spouse. If a premarital affair does occur, a marriage of the boy and girl must be considered. Aum.

SUTRA 224

My followers shall accept the serious responsibility of guiding the private and social life of their children. Parents chaperone and monitor friendships, thus ensuring that young ones remain celibate until marriage. Aum.

SUTRA 225

My followers shall require children to decide before age twenty whether to enter the fellowship, of their own volition, or to choose another path. If they go their own way, they are always welcome back. Aum Namasivaya.

Duties of Young Adults

SUTRA 226

All my followers who are adolescents shall use their aggressiveness, self-will and independence to bring converts into our religion and seekers into the fellowship, and to bring strayed members back into the fold. Aum.

SUTRA 227

My young adult followers must realize that they have a debt to their parents for their birth, early raising and education, which they pay by obedience and affection, giving joy, practical assistance and satisfaction. Aum.

SUTRA 228

All my young adult followers shall esteem their mother and father. In respecting their parents, they respect themselves and keep the doors open to parental aid and advice on the churning sea of adolescent experience. Aum.

SUTRA 229

My adolescent followers must hold their own among their peers and be leaders. To bend to peer pressure and offend the dharma shows weakness of character and parental neglect. Nothing but shame can follow. Aum.

SUTRA 230

All my young male followers are free to pursue their born destiny of either renunciation or family life. This choice of the two traditional paths is their birthright. Following either, they follow dharma. Aum Namasivaya.

Arranging Marriages

SUTRA 231

My followers shall arrange the marriages of their children, seeking sameness of lineage, astrological compatibility, harmony of families, total consent of both boy and girl and, foremost, the Satguru's blessings. Aum.

SUTRA 232

All my followers realize that forced marriages—those that overlook compatibility, the feelings of the couple or the guru's counsel—are not spiritually sound partnerships and require extra community support. Aum.

SUTRA 233

Weddings are a spiritual event among my followers. They are forbidden to engage in dowry payments or the exchange of prearranged excessive gifts. Nor shall marriage rites place a financial burden on the families. Aum.

SUTRA 234

My followers shall, before marriage, each prepare a written promise to the other, defining the duties, responsibilities and expectations of their life together. Every five years or less, this agreement is renewed. Aum.

SUTRA 235

Each marriage within the fellowship shall enjoy support, strength and encouragement from the Satguru and all followers, and counsel from elders when needed, especially during times of trial. Aum Namasivaya.

Sustaining Marriages

SUTRA 236

My followers shall look on their marriage as a spiritual partnership for the purpose of uplifting each other and bringing forth higher souls. It is a union not only of man and woman but of two entire families. Aum.

SUTRA 237

My married followers shall encourage their spouse to perform more daily spiritual disciplines, more religious service, more meditation and ritual worship. They are forbidden to discourage such noble practices. Aum.

SUTRA 238

My followers who are married should regulate their sex life according to traditional accepted practices and confine their affectionate looks to one another. They never hold hands, embrace, caress or kiss in public. Aum.

SUTRA 239

My followers are forbidden to commit adultery. They are further forbidden to steal the affections of another. They understand fidelity's power and know transgressions are rewarded by pain, guilt and remorse. Aum.

SUTRA 240

Followers who have raised their family may, by mutual consent and with guru's blessings, choose to live in celibacy, as brother and sister. In so doing, they transmute their vital energies into the divine. Aum Namasivaya.

About Divorce

SUTRA 241

In marriages of my followers, adultery, enduring abuse, severe neglect and abandonment may be cause for separation but never divorce. Spiritual law permits no divorce, and separation is looked upon as temporary. Aum.

SUTRA 242

In cases of divorce, the follower who forces the final divorce decree and thus ends the marriage is no longer a member of the fellowship. He or she should be shunned and urged to seek out a more lenient lineage. Aum.

SUTRA 243

Should a marriage among followers end in divorce, despite all efforts, the innocent spouse may remain in the fellowship. But he or she may not remarry and must uphold the continent life of service and devotion. Aum.

SUTRA 244

Any follower who has been divorced from a Hindu marriage must adopt the path of lifelong celibacy to join the ranks of the fellowship. Ancient tradition declares that to later remarry would result in dismissal. Aum.

SUTRA 245

Any non-Hindu follower sincerely seeking to enter the fellowship who has been divorced is permitted to remarry but only among the fellowship, provided he or she first becomes a Saivite Hindu. Aum Namasivaya.

Part Eight

Protocol

Devotion to the Satguru

SUTRA 246

All my followers shall daily offer gifts in love, and prostrate before their Satguru, or to his sandals or to the direction in which he abides. They chant the guru mantra when approaching any Satguru for darshan. Aum.

SUTRA 247

My followers should look upon their Satguru as the very embodiment of Lord Siva Himself, offering service and reverence equally to both, making no distinction between the two. Those who do are true followers. Aum.

SUTRA 248

All my followers must meditate each morning upon the inner form of their Satguru, striving to understand his temperament, the contents of his heart and his true nature, which is eternal, peaceful and unattached. Aum.

SUTRA 249

All followers must hasten to receive the leavings of their Satguru's food and the sanctified waters from his holy sandals. In serving the spiritual master, the whole world is served and dharma fulfilled that very moment. Aum.

SUTRA 250

All my followers should emulate the awakened qualities they see in their Satguru, seek initiation and strive to fathom his realization of Parasivam, which is his priceless gift, attainable by no other means. Aum Namasivaya.

Working with the Satguru

SUTRA 251

My followers shall seek the Satguru's blessings, act in harmony with his will, trust in his supreme wisdom, seek refuge in his grace, and rush forward to rededicate themselves yearly during the month of the guru. Aum.

SUTRA 252

All my followers must obey their Satguru and carry out his directions, expressed or implied, without delay or reservation. They keep no secrets from him, nor advise others about how to manipulate his decisions. Aum.

SUTRA 253

All my followers shall heed the Satguru's counsel without even subtly attempting to change his mind. Should he decline to give blessings for a project or enterprise, that is his blessing, and they proceed no further. Aum.

SUTRA 254

All my followers may undertake simple practices on their own, but serious penance and rigorous discipline must come directly from the Satguru. Severe austerities are for the initiated, at rare moments of life. Aum.

SUTRA 255

My followers shall upon the entrance or arrival of the Satguru, cease worldly activity and conversation. They rise and walk forward to greet him, offer him a seat of honor, then wait for instructions. Aum Namasivaya.

In the Satguru's Presence

SUTRA 256

My followers are forbidden by tradition to criticize their Satguru, even behind his back, or to argue with him, contradict or correct him. They may, however, request clarification and offer additional information. Aum.

SUTRA 257

In our heritage, all followers are forbidden to stand or sit above their Satguru, to walk or drive ahead of him, take a place of authority or instruct others in his presence. They are ever sensitive in his lofty company. Aum.

SUTRA 258

Followers must never utter words of falsehood or contempt before their Satguru. Nor shall they deceive him, address him as an equal, imitate him in dress or deportment or speak excessively in his holy presence. Aum.

SUTRA 259

When with the Satguru, followers neither initiate conversation nor ask questions unless invited. If he prefers silence, silence is the message, the nectar from the deep well of the Satguru's unspeakable unfoldment. Aum.

SUTRA 260

My followers never listen to criticism of their Satguru. If slander is heard, they extol the guru and warn the trespasser of his encroachment. If he persists in ignorance, they leave in eloquent silence. Aum Namasivaya.

Respecting Saints and Dignitaries

SUTRA 261

My followers shall prostrate before their Satguru and his successors, lightly touch the feet of his achariyas and swamis, and greet yogis and sadhakas with their palms pressed together and head slightly bowed. Aum.

SUTRA 262

Hearing of a venerated swami's arrival, my followers joyously rush to the outskirts of town to welcome him. On his departure, they accompany him there and, with gifts, money and good wishes, bid him farewell. Aum.

SUTRA 263

All my followers must duly honor a Satguru, a head of state, an elder, a learned one, a renunciate or ascetic of any lineage. Upon their entrance, my followers rush forward, bow appropriately and offer kind words. Aum.

SUTRA 264

My followers venerate and honor the rishis, Satgurus, gurus, saints and monastics of our tradition. Though they revere their own Satguru as Siva Himself, they do not worship anyone as an incarnation of Siva. Aum.

SUTRA 265

None of my followers should ever fail to gently touch the feet of a Satguru or holy man of any order dressed in saffron robes, but they need prostrate only to their own Satguru. This is the tradition. Aum Namasivaya.

Social Injunctions

SUTRA 266

My adult followers shall refrain from touching adolescents or adults of the opposite sex, other than near relatives or older persons. They do not embrace or shake hands except when required by social protocol. Aum.

SUTRA 267

All my followers who are no longer children should remain apart from the opposite sex when attending temples and public gatherings. Upon entering, women should sit on the left side, and men on the right. Aum.

SUTRA 268

No followers should garland members of the opposite sex other than their spouse or blood relatives. Women never garland a swami, yogi or sadhaka, but may during special ceremonies garland their own Satguru. Aum.

SUTRA 269

All followers must observe a period of thirty-one days following the birth or death of a family member during which they do not enter temples or home shrines, perform worship rites or attend auspicious events. Aum.

SUTRA 270

None of my followers shall recognize the Indian caste system or perpetuate its rules, foibles and restrictions. Instead, they base respect and status on attainment, knowledge and spiritual unfoldment. Aum Namasivaya.

Interfaith Harmony

SUTRA 271

My followers shall properly respect and address all virtuous persons of all religious traditions. They may support and participate in ecumenical gatherings from time to time with leaders and members of all faiths. Aum.

SUTRA 272

None of my followers should ever speak disrespectfully about other Hindu lineages, their Gods, sacred sites, scriptures or holy men and women, nor vilify other religions. They refuse to even listen to such talk. Aum.

SUTRA 273

My followers avoid the enchantment of other ways, be they ancient or modern. They remain friendly toward but aloof from other religions except when their members sincerely approach Hinduism for its wisdom. Aum.

SUTRA 274

All my followers realize that for eons our lineage has come forward to recreate a Hindu unity. Therefore, they are dedicated to building when necessary, and keeping strong when not, an invincible Hindu solidarity. Aum.

SUTRA 275

My followers, with hearts as big as the sky, love and accept Vaishnavas, Smartas and Saktas as brothers and sisters, even if not accepted by them, and maintain harmony by not discussing differences. Aum Namasivaya.

Avoiding Alien Influences

SUTRA 276

My followers are one-pointed in their striving on the path. They never join or study the courses of other religious, spiritual, esoteric, secular humanist, materialist, existentialist or "self-improvement" institutions. Aum.

SUTRA 277

Followers should never listen to discourses that might deter them from their commitment, devotion or duty unless willing and able to turn the detractor's mind around by debating the truths of Saiva Siddhanta. Aum.

SUTRA 278

None of my followers should ever educate their children in institutions that would force upon them the teachings of alien religions. They know that the impressions of youth go deep and can never be totally erased. Aum.

SUTRA 279

All my followers must stand strong and associate with devout Hindus whose beliefs are similar to their own and not mix with fundamentalist or liberal Hindus who would infiltrate, dilute and destroy their faith. Aum.

SUTRA 280

My followers know that everything they need in fulfillment of their path to Liberation is contained within this Nandinatha lineage. With the final conclusions in their grasp, they need look no further. Aum Namasivaya.

Part Nine

The Fellowship

Temples and Priesthood

SUTRA 281

My followers shall revere Kauai Aadheenam's Iraivan Temple as their center of the universe, all Saiva dharmasalas as sites of learning and service, and guru mandrams as places of daily worship and assembly. Aum.

SUTRA 282

My followers shall, with the Satguru's blessings, build guru mandrams at local missions, Muruga temples at Saiva dharmasalas and Siva temples at our full-fledged aadheenams. Yea, they are all temple builders. Aum.

SUTRA 283

My followers recognize my monastics as their official priesthood. However, they may hire Sivachariya priests when needed for performing sacraments, conducting festivals, installing Deities and dedicating temples. Aum.

SUTRA 284

My followers shall perpetuate in all our temples the architecture outlined in the Saiva Agamas and exemplified in the sanctuaries of South India, to create truly holy places where even the stones have sanctity. Aum.

SUTRA 285

Followers worship at fellowship missions, dharmasalas and aadheenams and other Saivite temples. They do not attend temples of other denominations except during pilgrimage or when required socially. Aum Namasivaya.

Weekly Gatherings

SUTRA 286

All my followers shall organize themselves into local missions to nurture religious life through worship, family gatherings, sacraments and community service, in accordance with *The Saiva Dharma Shastras.* Aum.

SUTRA 287

Those of the fellowship must rush to their mission house for weekly satsang to worship devoutly and sing loudly in praise of God, Gods and guru. They gather at local public temples for all the major Saivite festivals. Aum.

SUTRA 288

At gatherings among themselves, my followers shall sing *Natchintanai* exclusively and ponder the deep meaning of Sage Yogaswami's sweet hymns. Whenever nonfollowers are present, other songs may be included. Aum.

SUTRA 289

All followers present at official fellowship meetings must unanimously agree and obtain the Satguru's blessings before finalizing any project. No votes are taken based on the majority superseding the minority. Aum.

SUTRA 290

My followers are forbidden to apply the principle of unanimous agreement to sovereign edicts issued from the Aadheenam's seat of power. Such proclamations are the uncontestable law of the Satguru. Aum Namasivaya.

Guidelines for Business

SUTRA 291

My followers may employ other followers in their business and are permitted to form partnerships or corporations one with another. By looking after the business of others as if it were their own, they shall prosper. Aum.

SUTRA 292

My followers never enter into business transactions without a written contract. In cases of dispute, fellowship members avoid courts of law and seek judgment from an arbitration board within the fellowship. Aum.

SUTRA 293

Individuals of the fellowship never borrow or lend money among themselves, even for interest, nor give any form of credit. They may do business one with another, but only through immediate cash transactions. Aum.

SUTRA 294

All my followers should treat servants and employees as they would members of their own family, never neglecting or taking advantage of them. They provide conditions that are safe, healthful and uplifting. Aum.

SUTRA 295

My followers never borrow from a monastery or temple. They may borrow belongings from other followers, provided such objects are returned within twenty-four hours after the purpose is fulfilled. Aum Namasivaya.

New Followers

SUTRA 296

All my followers shall reach out for new members by enthusiastically printing and distributing free religious literature and putting sacred texts of the lineage into libraries and educational institutions worldwide. Aum.

SUTRA 297

All those within the fellowship are stalwart and dedicated. Not one is half-hearted or equivocal. Each is a jewel, important to me and to each other. Thus, strictness is necessary when accepting new members. Aum.

SUTRA 298

All those within the fellowship shall accept newcomers as part of their own family. They care for, teach, guide, gently correct and prepare these souls for their first initiation. Yea, they too were once new members. Aum.

SUTRA 299

Those of the fellowship who sponsor new members shall be responsible for their strengths and failures during the probationary year, their study toward initiation and their merger with others as milk poured into milk. Aum.

SUTRA 300

My followers must search for those who are ripe to enter the monastery, realizing that the fellowship's core is its Saiva Siddhanta Yoga Order, and that many old souls are being born to perpetuate this lineage. Aum Namasivaya.

Conversion to Saivism

SUTRA 301

My followers shall relentlessly search for Saivite souls, finding them, drawing them to Siva and the Satguru and, when necessary, helping them convert to Saivism from the faiths or philosophies they have rejected. Aum.

SUTRA 302

All my followers must reach out to seekers who, half-converted, bear a Hindu first name. Gently they will assist them through a full and ethical conversion from all former faiths, then accept them wholeheartedly. Aum.

SUTRA 303

All my followers of other religions or lineages who seek to enter the fellowship must, with authorized guidance, formally sever all loyalties and commitments by talking with any former preceptors and gaining release. Aum.

SUTRA 304

My followers affirm that even seekers from within the Hindu fold must convert to enter our strict Saivite fellowship. All former commitments and memberships must be dissolved before new ones can be made. Aum.

SUTRA 305

My followers know that *conversion* means to change one belief structure into another and is never without some degree of fire and pain. Patient counseling is necessary through this soul-searching time. Aum Namasivaya.

Adversaries and Detractors

SUTRA 306

All my followers shall hold it their solemn duty to shun those who oppose, criticize or attack the fellowship. By not interacting with detractors, they forestall conflict and thus protect the fellowship and themselves. Aum.

SUTRA 307

All my followers realize that shunning means to courteously avoid, exclude, ignore and ostracize and thus build a firm wall of silence between the fellowship and its detractors, whether individuals or groups. Aum.

SUTRA 308

All followers who refuse to shun those who should be shunned should themselves be shunned. But none shall shun those who have reconciled with the preceptor and been publicly welcomed back into the fellowship. Aum.

SUTRA 309

My followers will extend every effort to welcome and bring back into the fellowship those seeking to reenter its fold, having formerly left, provided they show grief and remorse and repentance and fully reconcile. Aum.

SUTRA 310

All my followers should know that any monastic who abandons his vows and leaves the fellowship, or is dismissed, should be shunned, treated as an outsider, until he rights himself with his preceptor. Aum Namasivaya.

Raising Sons for the Monastery

SUTRA 311

Each fellowship family is commissioned to birth a son for the monastery. Prior to conception, parents shall mix with the swamis and pray to the Gods to bring through a soul destined to perpetuate the holy lineage. Aum.

SUTRA 312

Followers with sons inclined toward monastic life shall encourage these noble aspirations. Fathers and young sons should live as guests in the monastery periodically to nurture monastic patterns and tendencies. Aum.

SUTRA 313

My followers shall regard any son destined for the monastery not as their own child, but as the Satguru's progeny in their trusted care. All details of his training and education must be guided by the preceptor. Aum.

SUTRA 314

Followers with a monastic son are forbidden to claim special access or privileges based on blood ties. They never involve themselves in his life or through him the management of the fellowship. They stand apart. Aum.

SUTRA 315

Fellowship families must raise all sons to be worthy of entering my monastery for two years to serve, study and grow in character as they live the monk's selfless life. This is the ideal for all young men. Aum Namasivaya.

Part Ten

The Monastics

Monastic Holy Orders

SUTRA 316

All my monastics shall lead a steadfast, contented, humble life. Their purpose is contemplation upon and love of Siva, to maintain Siva consciousness, realize the Self and uplift others while serving their Satguru. Aum.

SUTRA 317

All my followers who are sadhakas and yogis uphold the four vows of humility, purity, confidence and obedience, renewable every two years. Swamis uphold for life these four and a fifth vow of renunciation. Aum.

SUTRA 318

My monastics shall never fail to take refuge in their God, their guru and their Great Oath. This is the highest path they have chosen, the culmination of numberless lives, perhaps the last in the cycle of reincarnation. Aum.

SUTRA 319

My monastics walk bravely into the future, letting go of the past and letting what is be. Through yoga their kundalini rises, expanding consciousness, changing values and creating magical happenings around them. Aum.

SUTRA 320

My monastics accept a selfless life in which all work their minds together, keeping the monastery strong. They never follow an individual path, nor remain remote or aloof from their brother monastics. Aum Namasivaya.

Monastic Mission

SUTRA 321

My monastics shall bring Saivism into the future of futures. The fullness of their mission lies in our three pillars of faith—temples, scriptures and Satgurus—which they are vowed to protect, preserve and promote. Aum.

SUTRA 322

My monastics never compromise their ideals or rules for material or political gain, nor ever come under the control of the wealthy or influential. They are forbidden to be told what to think, say or do except by their order. Aum.

SUTRA 323

My monastics are unfettered and fearless, wholeheartedly and boldly supporting the ancient Sanatana Dharma against all those who would infiltrate, dilute and destroy it. Yea, they are defenders of all Hindu sects. Aum.

SUTRA 324

All my monastics teach that God Siva is, and is in all things. They spread the light of the One Great God—the compassionate One, the One without a second, Lord of Lords, the Beginning and End of all that is. Aum.

SUTRA 325

All my monastics strive to keep Lord Siva foremost in their mind and heart, seeking pure emptiness. Like an unfilled bowl, devoid of ego, they are useful vessels for our supreme God's gracious will. Aum Namasivaya.

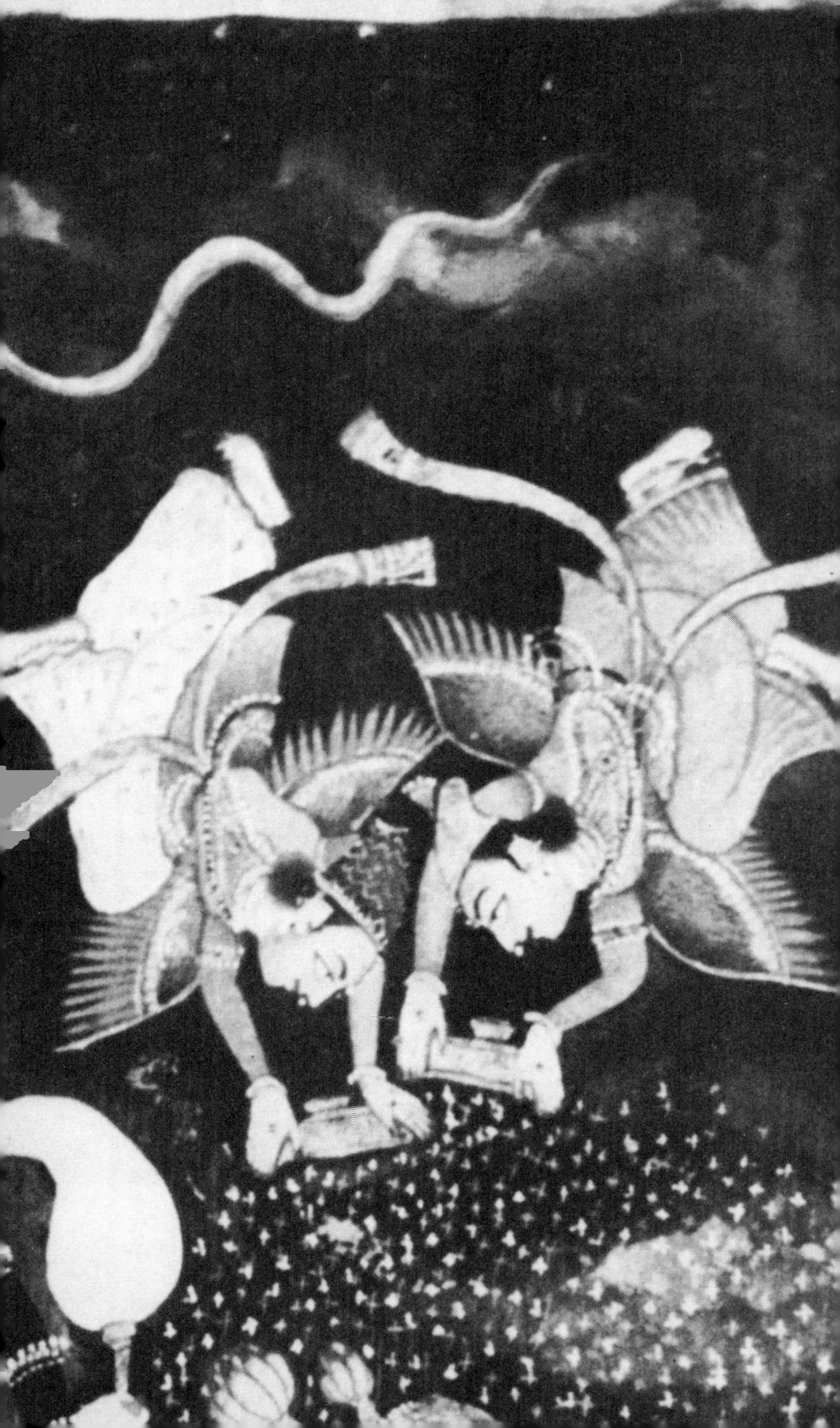

Monastic Spirit

SUTRA 326

All my monastics—achariyas, swamis, yogis and sadhakas—are precise, concentrated, serenely centered, eager to serve and tireless in every task, held back to rest only by others. Yea, they carry their yoga into action. Aum.

SUTRA 327

My monastics are strong-willed, soft in intellect, rushing forward in youthful, happy ways. Every desire they have is for the welfare of others. Yea, this group is the fellowship's core and has been for eons of time. Aum.

SUTRA 328

All my monastics who have separated themselves from family to pursue a divine life do so in a spirit of love. They look upon this not as losing their dear family of a few but as gaining all of humanity as their kin. Aum.

SUTRA 329

All my monastics follow the path of experiential yoga. They must never allow intellectual studies or interests to overshadow their spirituality. They are men of God first and teachers, scholars or artisans second. Aum.

SUTRA 330

All my monastics shall bear as their own karma all deprivations, insults and physical, mental or emotional beatings. They forgive inwardly at once, but outwardly only after transgressors reconcile. Aum Namasivaya.

Monastic Attitudes

SUTRA 331

My monastic followers shall regard themselves as the full-time slaves of Siva, servants of the servants of the Lord. They are masters of mind, body and emotion, divine rulers of their instinctive-intellectual forces. Aum.

SUTRA 332

My monastics are strong because they are challenged, productive because inwardly driven, steadfast because they are secure on the path they were born to follow, decisive because they are intuitive. Yea, they see. Aum.

SUTRA 333

My monastics must never look upon themselves as grander than any yogi, swami or guru of other orders. They serve all preceptors, promote their good causes, revere their efforts and enhance their names. Aum.

SUTRA 334

My monastics never boast about their knowledge, accomplishments, equipment, money they handle, places they have been or the people they know. Self-effacement—yea, self-erasement—is their hallmark. Aum.

SUTRA 335

My monastics regard sex, money, food and clothes as the prime challenge to their spiritual quest, harboring the magnetic potential to reinvolve them in the world. They restrain them accordingly. Aum Namasivaya.

Monastic Personal Care

SUTRA 336

My monastic followers shall wear robes that are cotton or wool, hand-spun, hand-woven and unsewn. Other clothing should be simple, unadorned cotton or wool, sewn in traditional North or South-Indian style. Aum.

SUTRA 337

My monastics observe the days of full moon, new moon and half moons and the day following each of these as periods of retreat for religious disciplines, personal care, ashram upkeep and beautification, study and rest. Aum.

SUTRA 338

My monastics sleep eight hours a day or less. Like all yogis before them, they refuse a soft bed and sleep on the floor or firm surface. This rule is suspended when ill or traveling. Not one is lenient with himself. Aum.

SUTRA 339

My monastics shall have no more belongings than what they can easily carry in two canvas bags, one in each hand. They own little, but even these few possessions they do not own. Yea, they are true mendicants. Aum.

SUTRA 340

My monastics look upon newcomers to the monasteries as they would their own children, to care for, tenderly nurture and train. They know it is their duty to pass on the wisdom of their years. Aum Namasivaya.

Monastic Travel and Retreat

SUTRA 341

My monastics shall not accept personal gifts of any kind, though they may receive donations on behalf of their monastery and support during pilgrimage, including fruit, flowers, food, lodging and travel expenses. Aum.

SUTRA 342

Monastics while traveling may stay in ashrams, temples, respectable hotels or in the homes of initiated fellowship families in good standing. Their stay, except in ashrams or hotels, must not exceed three nights. Aum.

SUTRA 343

Service to my monastic followers while in homes of initiated families, in temples or ashrams—such as meals, travel arrangements, laundry and visitors—shall be carried out by males. This is traditional protocol. Aum.

SUTRA 344

My monastics when traveling may eat in temples, ashrams, homes or restaurants, or cook for themselves. They are not restricted from eating in public places, whether the food is served by men or women. Aum.

SUTRA 345

My monastics, whether in or outside the monastery, perform ministry only in pairs. They may travel alone incognito, in seclusion, for up to nine days before they must be joined by another monastic. Aum Namasivaya.

Monastic Restrictions

SUTRA 346

All my monastics shall strictly avoid sexual fantasy, knowing it opens the door to the progressive stages of glorifying sex, flirting, desirous glances, love talk, pining, deciding to have sex and, finally, intercourse. Aum.

SUTRA 347

My monastics look at older women as their mother and younger women as their sisters. Intent on their renunciation, they are modest and reserved, avoiding extended conversation and exchange of subtle energies. Aum.

SUTRA 348

All my monastics firmly uphold the spirit of nonownership, never adopting the householder attitudes of claiming their own space, timing, tools, friends, ambitions, likes and dislikes. Yea, they are unattached. Aum.

SUTRA 349

All my monastics treasure harmony as their way of life. They stop work, attend to and resolve before sleep any inharmonious conditions that may arise, knowing that creativity lies dormant while conflict prevails. Aum.

SUTRA 350

My monastics who qualify may perform the parartha puja in our temples. However, should they not renew their vows or be dismissed, they are forbidden to perform or teach this puja thenceforth. Aum Namasivaya.

Monastics and the World

SUTRA 351

My monastics shall never allow themselves to be convinced or forced to act as go-betweens, messengers, agents, spies or bearers of false witness. They remain apart from all intrigue, corruption and cunning. Aum.

SUTRA 352

My monastics are commissioned to spiritual work and, except to advise and counsel, shall not concern themselves in secular events or social service. They do not vote or use their influence in the political arena. Aum.

SUTRA 353

My monastics follow the venerable tradition of not holding serious or lengthy private conversations with anyone without another monastic present. Gracious, impersonal small talk in public is, of course, allowed. Aum.

SUTRA 354

My monastics maintain a strict nontouching policy. They do not shake hands or embrace. However, if someone unfamiliar with this protocol initiates such contact, they do not recoil, but respond appropriately. Aum.

SUTRA 355

My monastics, in respect, stand no closer than an arm's length when holding a conversation. When speaking to men and women together, they direct their attention mostly to the men, as is traditional. Aum Namasivaya.

Instructions for Swamis

SUTRA 356

My swamis know that there is strength and guidance in orthodoxy and avoid the new for its own sake or because the old seems an arduous path. They uphold traditions which have survived the trials of time. Aum.

SUTRA 357

My swamis shall rigidly maintain the Nandinatha Sampradaya as independent and absolutely separate from the Smarta Dasanami orders and all other lineages. Yea, this autonomy shall endure until the end of time. Aum.

SUTRA 358

My followers who are swamis never speak of their past or personal self. Those who know tradition do not ask, for one should never look for the source of a rishi or a river. These always remain shrouded in mystery. Aum.

SUTRA 359

My swamis do not participate in births, weddings or other intimate householder events, but remain aloof from these activities. Nor do they attend funeral rites, except for those of brother monks and Satgurus. Aum.

SUTRA 360

All those in saffron robes who have braved death to the world are the brethren of my swamis, who appropriately honor respected male swamis older than themselves, touching their feet in homage. Aum Namasivaya.

Instructions for Achariyas

SUTRA 361

My followers who are achariyas are the supreme architects of the future of the fellowship and the fulfillers of these *Nandinatha Sutras.* They carry this responsibility on the top of their head. Yea, they are chosen ones. Aum.

SUTRA 362

All my followers who are achariyas shall realize that they are not beyond the laws of the land but must work within them even to the point of apologizing should misconduct occur on the part of the fellowship. Aum.

SUTRA 363

My followers who are achariyas nurture each devotee equally. They never make others their servants, order them about, shout at them, snap their fingers, clap their hands, strike or demean them at any time. Aum.

SUTRA 364

My followers who are achariyas are full of love and helpfulness, promoting joy and harmony among the fellowship. They never anger, never incite fear, nor take advantage of a person's health, wealth or well-being. Aum.

SUTRA 365

Numberless successors of the Nandinatha lineage have gone before me. Numberless shall follow. I have woven these 365 threads of wisdom, but there is infinitely more to know of the mysterious Nathas. Aum Namasivaya.

Conclusion

I HAVE THUS NARRATED SUCCINCTLY THE DUTIES AND DHARMA OF THE DIFFERENT CLASSES OF MY FOLLOWERS. THIS IS THE PATH OF THE Kailasa Parampara, which originated in the Himalayas and then spread to Chidambaram, Bangalore, Sri Lanka and Hawaii. Those who are not my followers are, as they read this book, looking through a window at an existing group of people born in an ancient tradition from parents raised by its precepts. They are viewing, as from a mountaintop, a race of spiritual seekers who were and are followers of the Maharishi Tirunandi, his disciple Tirumular and the countless gurus who succeeded them—the venerable Rishi from the Himalayas, the great Siddhar Kadaitswami, Satguru Chellappaswami, Sage Yogaswami and myself. What I have stated in these sutras merely defines the basics, and for further elaboration all should refer to our scriptures and *The Saiva Dharma Shastras.* Monastics should refer to the books of the five winds and their monastic vows. Those who live in accordance with the precepts laid down in the *Nandinatha Sutras* shall, with the grace of Siva and their Satguru, attain the four noble goals of duty, wealth, love and Liberation. Aum Namasivaya.

Glossary

aadheenam: A South-Indian Saivite monastery-temple complex.
abdicate: To give up formally; to surrender or repudiate.
Absolute: God, ultimate, transcendent Reality, Parasivam.
achariya: A swami of the Saiva Siddhanta Yoga Order, duly ordained, who has completed at least 24 years of monastic life.
acupuncture: System of treating disease by piercing the body with needles.
adage: An old saying that has been popularly accepted as truth.
adept: Highly skilled; expert.
Adi Sankara: Ninth-century guru of the Smarta Sampradaya; noted for his nondualistic Vedanta and for establishing liberal, eclectic Hindu worship.
admonition: A warning to correct some fault; a mild rebuke.
adulate: To praise and flatter highly.
adultery: Sex between a married person and someone not his or her spouse.
Advaita Siddhanta: Monistic-theistic philosophy based on the Saiva Agamas.
advaita: "Not two." Nonduality; monism; opposite of dvaita or dualism.
adversary: A person opposing or fighting another; opponent; enemy.
adversity: A state of misfortune, difficulty and trouble; the cause of such.
advocate: To speak or write in support of; be in favor of.
affliction: Pain; suffering; distress.
affluence: An abundance of riches; wealth; opulence.
Agamas: Revealed scriptures of many Hindu sects, first recorded in first millenium BCE. They detail yoga, the path of Liberation and temple worship.
ahimsa: The ethic of not harming others, physically, mentally or emotionally.
alchemistically: Associated with *alchemy*—a mystical form of chemistry which aims to transmute one thing into something different or better.
allopathy: Modern "western" medicine utilizing remedies that produce effects different from or opposite to those produced by the affliction.
amphetamines: A family of drugs: dangerous, habit-forming stimulants.
anava: The ego, sense of "I" and "mine," ignorance; separation from God.
Anbe Sivamayam Satyame Parasivam: Saivite affirmation of faith meaning: "God Siva is immanent love and transcendent reality."
antithesis: A contrast or opposition; the exact opposite.
Appar: "Father." Endearing name of Saint Tirunavukkarasu, South Indian Saivite saint of the seventh century CE.
archives: A place where materials having documentary interest, such as manuscripts or records, are kept; the material, etc., kept in these places.
Ardhanarisvara: "Half-female Lord." Lord Siva as the androgynous God.
arduous: Difficult; requiring much labor, energy or strain.

Aries: Literally, "ram;" constellation known as Mesha in Hindu astrology. The Hindu year begins with the month of Aries, around mid-April.
artha: Wealth righteously acquired; one of the four legitimate goals of life.
ascetic: One leading a life of contemplation and rigorous self-denial.
astral: Of the subtle, nonphysical sphere (astral plane) which exists between the physical and causal planes.
astral projection: Traveling in inner bodies through subtle nonphysical planes while the physical body remains still in sleep, trance or meditation.
astrological compatibility: Comparison of the astrological charts of a man and a woman to determine compatibility for marriage.
atmartha puja: See *Saiva atmartha puja.*
attire: Clothes, especially rich or fine apparel; finery.
aura: The field of colors and shapes emanating from each person's body.
Ayurveda: Holistic Hindu medicine using dietary-lifestyle adjustments, massage, balancing of three humors, internal cleansing, herbs and minerals.
barbiturates: Dangerous, habit-forming drugs—depressants, sedatives.
begrudgingly: To give with ill will or reluctance.
betoken: To be a token or sign of; indicate; show.
bhakti yoga: "Union through devotion." Devotional disciplines, worship, prayer, chanting and singing with the aim of awakening love in the heart.
bhojana mantra: A Sanskrit chant said before meals to give praise and thanks.
brahmachari: A male who has taken a vow of celibacy.
brahmacharini: A female who has taken a vow of celibacy.
brahmachariya: Sexual purity—restraint of lust and the instinctive nature.
caste: Indian hierarchical social system established in ancient times by Vedic brahmin priests, basing status on heredity and occupation.
chakra: Centers of force and consciousness within the inner bodies of man.
chaperone: To supervise young, unmarried people at gatherings or meetings.
Chellappaswami: "Wealthy father." Reclusive siddhar of the Kailasa Parampara; Satguru of Siva Yogaswami. Lived 1840–1915 in northern Sri Lanka.
Chidambaram: "Hall of Consciousness" or "Hall of Pure Knowledge." An ancient and highly venerated Siva Nataraja temple in South India.
chiropractic: Medical therapy employing manipulation of the body joints, especially of the spine, to restore normal nerve function.
clairaudience: Psychic hearing. Hearing in one's mind the communication of inner plane beings, or beings on the physical plane.
clairvoyance: Psychic sight; seeing into inner worlds, perceiving auras, chakras, the past or future, forms of the astral or superconscious realms.
cocaine: A crystalline alkaloid obtained from dried cocoa leaves; a local anesthetic and a dangerous, addictive stimulant.
coffer: A chest or strongbox in which money or valuables are kept.
compromise: A settlement in which each side gives up some demands or makes concessions; a weakening, as of one's principles.

concoction: A compound made by combining various ingredients.
contemplative: Inclined toward a spiritual, religious, meditative way of life.
contempt: Attitude that considers someone or something as low, worthless.
continence: Total abstinence from sexual activity.
contradiction: A statement in opposition to another; denial; a condition in which things tend to be contrary to each other.
convert: To change from one religion or philosophy to another. One who has so changed, as in: "He is a *convert.* We helped him *convert.*"
crown chakra: The seventh subtle force center, located at the top of the head. Called *sahasrara* in Sanskrit, the seat of transcendental consciousness.
darshan: "Auspicious sight." Vision of the divine, physically or psychically; can refer to the seeing of a temple image, or a holy person or place.
Dasanami: Literally, "ten-fold." See: *Smarta Dasanami orders.*
decorum: Propriety and good taste in behavior, speech, dress, etc.
demean: To lower in status or character; degrade.
demureness: Decorous; modest; shy; reserved.
denomination: A specific division within a single religion; sect.
deprivations: Forced conditions of loss or neediness.
deter: To keep one from doing something by instilling fear, anxiety, doubt, etc.
detractor: One who discredits, slanders or disparages someone else.
devas: "Shining ones." Higher astral plane beings. Angels.
dharma: Divine law; righteousness; action in accordance with divine law.
diaspora: The dispersion of people with a common origin, background, beliefs, etc., such as the distribution of Jews when driven out of Israel.
dilute: To change or weaken by mixing with something else.
disdain: To regard or treat as unworthy or beneath one's dignity.
divisive: Causing division, especially causing disagreement or dissension.
dowry: Property a woman brings to her husband and his family at marriage as a condition upon which they will marry.
dualism: Opposite of monism. Any doctrine which holds that there are two eternal and distinct realities in the universe, e.g., God-world, good-evil.
ecumenical: Promoting cooperation or understanding among religions.
edict: An official public order issued by an authority.
effulgent: Having great brightness; radiance; brilliant; full of light.
eloquent: Vivid, forceful, fluent, graceful and persuasive speech or writing.
emulate: To try to equal or surpass, often by imitating or copying.
enchantment: A magic spell; a bewitching, captivating power.
encroachment: Gradual or sneaking trespass or intrusion.
endangered: On the verge of extinction, as of rare plants or animals.
enmity: Bitter attitude or feelings of an enemy; hostility; antagonism.
entanglements: Involvements in difficulty; being tangled or confused.
equivalent: Equal in value, force or meaning.
equivocal: Uncertain; undecided; doubtful.

esoteric: Beyond the understanding of all but a few, or the initiated.
exemplify: To show by being an example of.
existentialist: Adjective of "existentialism"—the doctrine that concrete individual existence takes precedence over abstract, conceptual essence.
expediency: Doing what is advantageous rather than what is right or just.
exploitative: Making unethical use of for advantage or profit.
extol: To praise highly; laud.
extravagant: Going beyond the reasonable limits; excessive, unrestrained.
fathom: To understand thoroughly the depths of.
favoritism: Showing more kindness to some persons than to others.
fellowship: Another word for the membership of Saiva Siddhanta Church.
fidelity: Faithfulness; having sexual relations only with one's spouse.
follower: All those who are influenced by the lineage, Nandinatha Sampradaya, and observe its teachings, including seekers, students, close devotees, readers of *Hinduism Today,* and all the many who come for darshan.
forfeiting: Giving up something due to a crime or fault or neglect of duty.
frugal: Not wasteful; not spending freely or unnecessarily; thrifty.
fundamentalist: One who interprets scripture literally; religious fanatic.
Ganesha: Elephant-faced God always worshiped first to remove obstacles.
Gangetic: Near to or on the banks of the Ganges river in North India.
guru mandram: A family-managed mission facility of Saiva Siddhanta Church.
guru mantra: Vedic chant praising the greatness of enlightened sages.
harassment: Trouble, worry or torment.
hasten: To move or act swiftly; hurry; to quicken.
hatha yoga: "Sun-moon yoga." Manipulating the body with specific postures.
heed: To pay close attention to; take careful notice of.
heroin: A powerful, habit-forming narcotic drug derived from morphine.
Himalayan Academy: The educational institution of Saiva Siddhanta Church, founded by Sivaya Subramuniyaswami in 1957.
Hinduism Today: The international, English, monthly newspaper published by Himalayan Academy and founded in 1979 by Sivaya Subramuniyaswami.
homeopathy: Medical system using minute doses of drugs that in larger amounts would produce symptoms of the respective disease.
humiliate: To hurt the pride or dignity of by causing to appear foolish.
immanent: Present throughout the universe.
impropriety: Improper action or behavior.
incarnation: Endowment with a human body. "Incarnation of Siva" means the taking of human birth by the Supreme Being.
incognito: Having one's true identity unrevealed or disguised.
indomitable: Not easily discouraged, defeated or subdued; unyielding.
infiltrate: To gradually penetrate so as to attack or seize control from within.
initiation: Act or rite entering one into new knowledge and practice.
injunction: Commands, orders, rules of what not to do.

inscrutable: Not easily understood; completely obscure or mysterious.
intrigue: Secret or underhanded plotting or scheming.
intrinsic: Belonging to the real nature of a thing; essential; inherent.
invincible: That which cannot be overcome; unconquerable.
Iraivan: "He who is worshiped or divine." Ancient Tamil name for Siva.
Jai: "Victory!"
japa: Repetition of a mantra (sacred syllable) as a devotional practice.
jurisdiction: A sphere of authority; the territorial range of authority.
Kadaitswami: "Marketplace swami." A siddhar of the Kailasa Parampara (circa 1770–1840); Satguru of Chellappaswami.
Kali Yuga: "Dark Age;" fourth and present age in the universe's four-phased time cycle, when ignorance is in power and soul faculties are obscured.
karma: "Deed or act." The principle of cause and effect; the totality of one's actions and their corresponding reactions in this and all previous lives.
Kauai: Northernmost of the Hawaiian islands; 555 sq. mi., pop. 50,000.
Kauai Aadheenam: Monastery-temple complex founded by Sivaya Subramuniyaswami in 1970; international headquarters of Saiva Siddhanta Church.
kavadi: Penance invoking Muruga's grace, carrying two pots of milk over the shoulders with a pole; may include piercing the flesh with hooks or spears.
Kumbalavalai: Famous Ganesha temple in Jaffna (northern Sri Lanka).
kundalini: The cosmic energy lying coiled at the base of the spine.
Liberation: Moksha; release from samsara (the round of births and deaths).
lineage: Line of succession of preceptors, each one initiating the next. In these sutras, lineage refers to the Nandinatha Sampradaya.
Lingam: "Mark of Siva." Rounded, elliptical image representing God Siva.
longevity: Long life; great span of life.
Lord Subramaniam Shastras: Akashic writings by Sivaya Subramuniyaswami detailing monastic traditions and early history of the planet.
lottery: Game of chance in which people buy numbered tickets, and prizes are given to those whose numbers are drawn by lot.
lucid dreaming: Being totally conscious in a dream.
Madurai: City in the South Indian state of Tamil Nadu; home of one of the world's most spectacular Saivite temples, called Meenakshi-Sundareswara.
magic: Use of charms, spells and rituals in seeking or pretending to cause or control events, or govern certain natural or supernatural forces.
Maha Sivaratri: "Siva's great night." The new moon in February-March and the year's darkest night; the most sacred Saivite festival, on which devotees observe an all-night fast and sleepless vigil in adoration of God Siva.
Mahadeva: "Great deva." A name of Siva. Also denotes any of the Gods.
maharishi: "Great rishi." Old, venerated Hindu sage or seer.
Manikkavasagar: Ninth-century Saivite saint who wrote *Tiruvasagam*.
mantra: Sacred syllable or verse used for meditation, japa or ritual.

materialist: One who believes that physical comfort, pleasure and wealth are the only or the highest goals of life, that matter is the only reality.
maya: The principle of matter; the world of manifest, changing form.
mead: Wine made from the simple fermentation of water and honey.
Meenakshi: "Fish-eyed." Names Sakti as the ever vigilant Divine Mother.
mendicant: A monk with no possessions who lives by begging.
menses: Monthly discharge from a woman's uterus.
mentor: One who advises, teaches, instructs, either formally or informally.
microbe: Microscopic life form, especially a bacteria that causes disease.
microscopic: So small as to be invisible except through a microscope.
millennia: Period of 1,000 years.
mind-reading: Perceiving another's thoughts without verbal communication.
mission house: A family home where members of a local Saiva Siddhanta Church mission gather for weekly satsang.
Moksha: A state of being free from the necessity of taking rebirth.
monistic theism: Doctrine that God Siva is one with the soul and all existence, and yet exists as a real, conscious, personal Supreme Being.
monistic: Expressive of the belief that reality is of one kind or substance.
mors voluntaria religiosa: Self-willed, religious death through fasting.
mridangam: A particular kind of two-headed South Indian drum.
Muruga: A Mahadeva, son of Siva, also called *Skanda, Palani* and *Kartikkeya.*
namaskaram: "Salutations." "I bow to the divine within you." Traditional Sanskrit greeting of respect. Equivalent to *namaste* and *vanakkam.*
namaste: The Hindi equivalent of *namaskaram.*
Nandinatha: Satguru of Tirumular; first-known Himalayan preceptor of the lineage of the Southern Natha tradition of Saivism.
Nataraja: God Siva as "King of the Dance."
Natchintanai: "Good thoughts." The songs and verses of Sage Yogaswami.
Natha Yoga Sutras: Refers to Patanjali's yoga aphorisms.
naturopathy: Treating diseases by natural means, rejecting the use of drugs.
nicotine: The addictive, water-soluble alkaloid found in tobacco leaves.
niyamas: "To unleash." Ten ethical and religious practices and observances comprising the third limb of the ashtanga ("eight-limbed") yoga system.
nondualism: "Not two." Refers to monistic philosophy. See: *Monism.*
nurture: To raise or promote development, train; educate or foster.
obscurity: Something not clear; faint or undefined; not easily understood.
occult: Hidden, concealed, secret, esoteric.
ostracize: Exclusion, by general consent, from a group.
palmist: One who reads characters or futures from the palm of the hand.
Panchakshara: "Five-lettered chant." Refers to *Namasivaya,* "Adoration (or homage) to Siva," the supreme mantra of Saivism.
paramount: Ranking higher than any other in importance.
parartha puja: Ancient Sanskrit liturgy performed by priests in Saivite temples.

Parasivam: "Transcendent Siva." Siva's Absolute Reality. That which transcends time, form and space and defies description; the Self God.
parliamentarians: Political leaders or important people in government.
Patanjali: Great Natha sage who codified the essential teachings of the eight-limbed Raja yoga in the famous text *Yoga Sutras.*
perpetuate: Cause to continue or be remembered; to keep from being lost.
pornography: Writings, pictures, etc., intended to arouse sexual desire.
pouting: Making a face showing sullenness or displeasure; to sulk.
precept: A commandment meant as a rule of action or conduct.
preceptor: Highly respected teacher and head of a spiritual order and clan; the equivalent of the word *Satguru.*
predator: Any being that captures other creatures to eat their flesh.
Primal Soul: The uncreated, original, perfect Soul—Siva—who emanates from Himself all universes and an infinite plurality of individual souls.
Primal Substance: The material form from which the manifest world is derived. The substance is Pure Consciousness, God Siva's Divine Mind.
progeny: Children, descendants or offspring collectively.
promiscuity: Indiscriminate sexual intercourse or sex with many persons.
protocol: A code of ceremonial forms and courtesies; correct behavior.
provocative: Stimulating, erotic, irritating.
psychic: Of the soul; perceiving beyond natural or known physical processes.
puberty: Time in youth when sexual capacity and characteristics develop.
Pure Consciousness: Satchidananda; Siva's Divine Mind. The ground state of Being which contains and underlies all form, time and space.
quantum level: Subtle sphere of existence, at or near the nuclear level.
quatrain: A stanza or poem of four lines.
quell: To quiet, subdue or put an end to.
raja yoga: The eight-limbed, meditative yoga of Patanjali's *Yoga Sutras.*
reconciliation: To harmonize subtle quarrels or mend differences. A tithing reconciliation is a written accounting of income and tithing.
regenerative: Bringing into existence again; reestablishing on a new basis.
reincarnate: Taking birth in another body, having lived and died before.
remorse: Deep sense of guilt or regret felt over a wrong that one has committed.
renunciate: One who has given up worldly life; a monk.
reprimand: A severe or formal rebuke, especially by a person in authority.
rishi: Old, venerated sage or seer, often a visionary of the future.
rowdy: Rough, quarrelsome and disorderly.
rudraksha: "Eye of Siva." Marble-sized, multi-faced, reddish-brown seeds from the species *eleocarpus ganitrus*; in English called the blue marble tree.
sacrament: A rite that carries a spiritual blessing or sacred mystical meaning.
sadhaka: An aspirant who performs religious service and spiritual disciplines.
Saiva Atmartha Puja: Sanskrit liturgy performed in the home shrine.
Saiva Dharma Shastras: Saiva Siddhanta Church's *Book of Discipline,* detail-

ing policies, membership rules and mission operations.

Saiva dharmasala: A Himalayan Academy monastery-temple complex staffed by monastics of Saiva Siddhanta Church.

Saiva Siddhanta Church: "Church of God Siva's Revealed Truth," founded in 1949 by Sivaya Subramuniyaswami.

Saiva Siddhanta Yoga Order: Ecclesiastical body of lifetime renunciate swamis. This sangam was founded by Sivaya Subramuniyaswami in 1949.

Saiva Siddhanta: Saivism's largest denomination; a monistic-theistic philosophy and religious way of life based on the Vedas and Saiva Agamas. There are two schools, Meykandar's pluralism and Tirumular's monism.

Saktas: Those who worship Goddess Sakti as the Supreme.

Sakti: "Power, energy." The active power of Siva (or other Deities), interpreted as a feminine force or Goddess, such as Parvati, Meenakshi and Lakshmi.

samadhi: "Sameness; union." Eighth step of ashtanga yoga. Total absorption of individual awareness in deep, contemplative meditation.

Sambandar: Child saint of the 7th century Saivite renaissance in South India.

sampradaya: "Tradition." An historical lineage; a living stream of tradition or theology within Hinduism, passed on by oral initiation and training.

Sanatana Dharma: "Eternal religion" or "eternal path;" the oldest name for the Hindu religion.

sandalpaste: A yellow paste made from the heart of the sandalwood tree.

Sankara: A name of Siva, meaning "author of knowledge." See: *Adi Sankara.*

sannyasin: A Hindu monk, properly initiated, who has renounced the world.

Sanskrit: The classical religious language of India.

Satguru: A spiritual master of the highest calibre. An enlightened soul who has realized the ultimate truth and can magically transmit it to others.

secular humanism: A system that rejects religious faith and worship and holds that one need not look beyond man for life's ethical meaning.

secular: Not sacred or religious; temporal or worldly.

self-effacement: Modest, retiring behavior; giving all credit to God, preceptor and other persons and not accepting praise for one's accomplishments.

self-erasement: The process of wiping out or eradicating the personal ego and the dross of the past, lodged in the memory patterns of the subconscious.

sepulcher: A burial vault; grave; tomb. In Sanskrit, known as a *samadhi.*

shanti mantra: "Peace chant." A Vedic verse invoking harmony among all.

shirk: To neglect or evade doing something that should be done.

shrouded: Covered, protected, screened, veiled, sheltered.

Shum: An esoteric language revealed in Switzerland in 1968 by Sivaya Subramuniyaswami, used for meditative exploration. Its script looks like this:

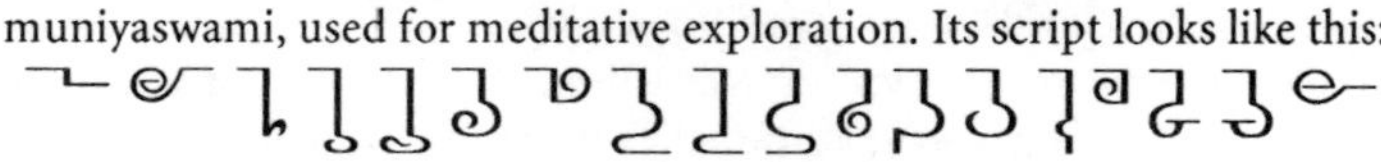

shun: To keep away from; ignore or avoid scrupulously or consistently.

Siddhanta: "Final Attainments" or "final conclusions." The ultimate understanding arrived at in any given field of knowledge.

Siva-Sakti: Father-Mother God; both immanent and transcendent. A name for God Siva encompassing His unmanifest Being and generative power.

Sivachariya: The original hereditary priesthood ordained to perform the daily rites of worship in Siva temples.

Sivaya: "To Siva."

Smarta Dasanami orders: Ten liberal orders of sannyasins formalized by Adi Sankara, 9th century. In general, these orders support the Indian caste system and oppose orthodox sectarianism: Saivism, Vaishnavism and Saktism.

Smarta: Originally a liberal Indian brahminical caste that borrowed from orthodox traditions, now a liberal Hindu lineage with five regional pontifs.

solitaire: One who lives alone; a hermit or anchorite.

stalwart: Strong, well-built; brave; valiant; resolute; firm; unyielding.

stewards: Those responsible to administrate or care for another's property.

sub-subconscious: Area of the subconscious where past experiences mix and merge, forming new images, reactions and beliefs.

subjugate: To bring under control or subjection.

Subramuniya: A name of Muruga: *subra* meaning "superconscious knowledge and light," and *muni*, "a silent sage who teaches through intuition."

substratum: A substance or element which lies beneath and supports another.

subsuperconscious: Insight, creativity. A state of mind bringing intuition, perfect timing, creative breakthroughs, extrasensory perception.

succinctly: Clearly and briefly stated.

Suddha Saiva Siddhanta: "Pure Saiva Siddhanta." A philosophy encompassing monism and theism, Vedas and Agamas, Vedanta and Siddhanta, as distinguished from pluralistic Saiva Siddhanta.

Sundarar: Saint of the 9th century who helped in the Saivite renaissance.

sutra: "Thread." A short verse or statement conveying specialized knowledge.

swami: "He who knows himself." Title for a Hindu holy man, usually a sannyasin—one who has taken lifetime time vows of renunciation.

tambura: Indian stringed instrument which sounds three drone notes.

Tamil: A Dravidian language and Caucasian race of South India.

tenet: A principle, doctrine, or belief held as a truth, as by some group.

Thayumanavar: A famous South Indian Saivite saint of the 18th century.

theism: Belief that God exists as a real, conscious, personal Supreme Being.

Tirukural: "Holy Couplets." An ethical, moral scripture written by Saint Tiruvalluvar; 1,330 verses on conduct and human experience.

Tirumantiram: "Holy mantras." The Nandinatha Sampradaya's oldest Tamil scripture; written *circa* 200 BCE by Rishi Tirumular.

Tirumular: Nandinatha Sampradaya sage and yogi who journeyed from the Himalayas *(circa* 200 BCE) to Tamil Nadu and composed the *Tirumantiram.*

tiruvadi: The feet of the Satguru or his holy sandals. The guru's feet are especially sacred, being the point of contact of the divine and physical spheres.

Tiruvalluvar: Householder weaver saint, author of *Tirukural.*
trance mediumship: The practice of going into trance and allowing inner-plane beings to speak through oneself as a medium; also called channeling.
trance: Altered state of consciousness somewhat resembling sleep during which voluntary movement is lost, as in hypnosis.
transcendent: Attribute or perfection of God; beyond the limits of; prior to or beyond; existing apart from the material universe.
trespasser: One who goes beyond the limits of what is considered right.
tribulation: Great misery or distress, as from oppression; deep sorrow.
Tyaf: A language revealed in Paris in 1974 by Sivaya Subramuniyaswami used especially for communication with inner-plane beings by burning prayers in the sacred temple fire. The Tyaf alphabet looks like this:

unambiguously: Clearly; with certainty; having only one meaning.
unscrupulous: Not restrained by ideas of right and wrong; unprincipled.
unwavering: Not having any doubt or indecision.
Vaishnavas: Those who worship the Supreme as Vishnu or any of the incarnations of Vishnu, such as Krishna or Rama.
vanakkam: The Tamil equivalent to *namaskaram.*
Vedanta: "Final conclusions of the Vedas." The philosophy embodied in the Upanishads—the philosophical portion of the Vedas.
veena: Large South Indian stringed instrument with gourds on either end.
Vel: "Spear, lance." The symbol of Lord Muruga's divine authority.
venerate: To look upon with feelings of deep respect or reverence.
vilify: To use abusive or slanderous language against; to revile or defame.
yea: Yes, indeed, truly, verily. Not only that, but more.
Yoga Sutras: A scripture composed by Sage Patanjali over 2,000 years ago codifying in terse verses the essential teachings and methods of yoga.
yoga: "To yoke or unite." Connotes the process of yoking or fusing individual consciousness with the Divine and the method to achieve this union.
Yogaswami: Sri Lanka's renowned spiritual master (1872–1964); siddhar of the Kailasa Parampara who initiated Sivaya Subramuniyaswami in 1949.

Index

aadheenam(s), 47, 131, 133
Absolute, 29
abundance, 71
abuse, 99, 111
accounting, 69, 101
accusation, 85
achariya(s), vii, xi-xii, 43, 121, 151, 165
acquaintances, 95
acupuncture, 55
addictive, 57
addicts, 23
adept, 45
adolescent(s), 91, 105, 123
adultery, 109, 111
advaita, 29
Advaita Siddhanta, 29
adversity, 21
advice, xi, 27, 43, 105
advise, 117, 161
advocate, 73
affair, 103
affection(s), 105, 109
affirm, 139
affirmation(s), 33, 41, 49, 101
afflictions, 43
affluence, 69
Agamas, 27, 131
aged, 95
agents, 161
aggressiveness, 105
ahimsa, v, 15, 17
alchemistically, 77
alcohol(s), vi, 59
alien, vii, 127
allopathy, 55
allowance, 101
amorous, 21
amphetamines, 57
anava, 31
Anbe Sivamayam Satyame Parasivam, 33, 49
ancestors, 65
anger, 9, 45, 85, 99, 165
animal(s), ix, 3, 19
anniversary, iii
annual love-offering, 71
antagonize, 81
apologizing, 165
Appar, 27
appetite, 11
arbitration, 135
architecture, 131
archives, 95
Ardhanarisvara, 37
arduous, 163
argue, 81, 119
Aries, 39
arise, xii, 45, 87, 159
arrival, 81, 103, 117, 121
art(s), 39, 43, 55, 99
artisans, 151
ascetic(s), 53, 95, 121
ash(s), 45, 49, 65, 89
ashram(s), 155, 157
Asian, x, 39
assembly, 131
associate, 23, 81, 83, 85, 87, 127
associations, 83, 87
astral bodies, 31
astral projection, 43
astrological compatibility, 107
astrology, 43, 89, 99, 107
atheists, 23
atmartha puja, 37
atone, 47
attachments, 5, 41
attack, 141
attainment(s), iii, xii, 89, 123, 167
attend, 81, 123, 131, 159, 163
attire, 81
attitude(s), vii, xiii, 39, 99, 153, 159
aura, 41
auspicious, 3, 39, 97, 123
austerity, 13, 117
authority, 27, 119
authorized, v, xii, 27, 37, 139
autonomy, 163
autopsy, 65
avoid, vii, xiii, 11, 19, 21, 53, 57, 63, 83, 85, 97, 125, 127, 135, 141, 159, 163
awaken, 47, 49, 57, 115
ayurveda, 53, 55
backbiting, 15
bacteria, 17
Bangalore, 167
barbiturates, 57
bathe, 45, 81, 87
bead(s), 13, 49, 89
beat, 85, 151
beautification, 155
beauty, xiii, 47
bed(s), 47, 155
being, xiii, 3, 13, 19, 29, 41, 137
belief(s), v, xiii, 25, 27, 29, 31, 33, 127, 139
bhakti, 45
bhojana mantra, 49
bible, 27
birth(s), xi, 63, 105, 123, 143, 163
birthright, 105

bliss, 29
boast, 23, 153
bodies, 31, 41
book(s), ii, xiii, 71, 167
borrow, 135
boys, 49, 99
brahmachari(s), xi, 91
brahmacharini(s), xi, 91
breasts, 85
brethren, 163
bribes, 23
builders, 131
business, vii, xi, 69, 101, 103, 135
calendar, 39
career, 101
caress, 109
caring, 57
cash, 135
caste, 19, 123
catechism, 27
causal plane, 31, 65
celibate, 11, 21, 89, 91, 103, 109, 111
centers, 41
ceremony(s), 39, 65, 95, 123
chakra(s), 41, 57, 63, 89
challenge(s), v, xii, 5, 75, 153
chance, 23
chant, 13, 45, 47, 49, 115
chaperone, 103
chastity, 91, 103
Chellappaswami, 167
chemical, 57
chemistry, 55
chiropractic, 55
citadel, 37
citizens, 19
civic, 17
clairaudience, 43
clairvoyance, 43
clarification(s), xii, 119
class(s), 167
classical, v, 7, 11, 13
clean, 45, 47, 65
clear white light, 9, 63
clothes, 45, 89, 95, 153, 155
coaching, xii
cocaine, 57
coffer, 47
cognition, 13
college, 101
commitment(s), xii, 127, 139
community, xi, 7, 15, 17, 39, 57, 73, 89, 107, 133
company, 83, 119
compassion, x, 9, 11, 15, 31, 33, 95, 149
compatible, 89, 107
competition, 7
complaining, 9
complaint, 5
compromise, 77, 149
concealing, 49
conception, 143
concoctions, 57
conflict, 141, 159
conflicting, ix
confusion, iii, ix-x, 57
conscience, ix, 7
consciousness, ix, 3, 5, 29, 41, 45, 55, 63, 71, 81, 147
conservative, 19, 77
console, 99
contemplative, 5
contempt, 9, 119
continence, 89, 111
conversation(s), 81, 85, 117, 119, 159, 161
conversion, vii, 139
convert(s), 105, 139
cook, 53, 99, 157
corporations, 135
corruption, 75, 161
cosmetics, 89
costumes, 85
cotton, 155
counsel, 61, 99, 107, 117, 161
counseling, 63, 139
courses, 127
coveting, 11
craft, 39
creator, 29, iii
creature(s), ix, 15, 17, 19
credit, 135
creed, xiii, 19, 27
cremation, 65
crown chakra, 63
cuisine, 53
culture, xi, xiii, 57, 85
cultures, 19, 49, 53
custom(s), 39, 47, 49, 59
daily, x, 5, 7, 13, 39, 45, 83, 109, 115, 131
dance, 3, 29, 39
darshan, 115
Dasanami, 163
dawn, 45
death, vi, xi, 63, 65, 77, 123, 163
debate, 95, 127
debt, 11, 105
deceive, 119
deception, 11
decorum, 59
decree, 111
deities, 131
demonic music, 57
demureness, 59
denominations, 131
departure, 121
deprivations, 151
desire(s), 9, 45, 83, 101, 151
desirous, 159
detractor(s), vii, 127, 141
devas, 39, 43
devotion, vii, 13, 23, 91, 111, 115, 127, 133
dharma, ii-iii, 61, 85, 95, 97, 103, 105, 115, 133, 149, 167
dharmasalas, 131

diet, 53, 55, vi
dignitaries, vii, 121
dilute, 127, 149
disdain, 85
disease-carrying, 17
disharmony, 7
dismissal, 111
dismissed, 141, 159
disobedience, 101
dispute(s), xi-xii, 135
divisive, 73
divorce, vi, xi, 83, 87, 111
divorcee(s)xi, 83
divorcé, xi, 87
doctor, 55
dowry(s), 107
dream(s), xii, 11, 43
dress, 39, 81, 85, 119
drug culture, 57
drug(s), vi, 57
dualism, 29
ear-piercing, 99
eating, 11, 53, 157
ecumenical, 125
edicts, 133
ego, 149
eightfold, 21
elder(s), xii, 59, 61, 97, 99, 107, 121
elderly, 97
embalming, 65
emotion(s), 5, 15, 21, 41, 53, 59, 61, 85, 151, 153
employ, 85, 135
employees, 135
endangered plants or animals, 19
endowments, 61, 71
enemies, 63
enlightened, xii
enlightenment, 13, 41
enmity, 75
entanglements, 97
environment, v, 19, 47, 73
ethnic, xi
evil, v, 33
exercise, vi, 11, 55
existentialist, 127
expenditures, 101
expense(s), 69, 71, 157
exploitative, 73
exploited species, 19
eyes, ix, 81
family home evening, 83
fantasy, 21, 159
fast, 15, 53
favoritism, 75
fear(s), xiii, 5, 9, 11, 15, 57, 61, 99, 149, 165
fearless, 149
fellowship, vii, 29, 37, 43, 59, 61, 69, 91, 103, 105, 107, 111, 129, 131, 133, 135, 137, 139, 141, 143, 151, 157, 165
festival(s), 47, 131, 133
fidelity, 109
financial, 77, 101, 107
five states of mind, 41
flirtation, 21, 159
flowers, 89, 157
food(s), vi, 19, 53, 55, 65, 95, 115, 153, 157
forbidden, 15, 37, 57, 59, 65, 77, 99, 107, 109, 119, 133, 143, 149, 159
forehead dot, 89
forgive, 63, 151
freedom(s), 75
fundamentalist, 127
funeral, 65, 99, 163
gambling, 23
Ganesha, 31, 37
garden, xiii, 17, 39
garland, 123
gathering(s), vii, 95, 123, 125, 133
generation(s), xi, 61
gestures, 39
gift(s), 107, 115, 121, 157
giving, 5, 13, 105
God-Realization, 3
grace, iii, 31, 33, 117, 167
graft, 75
guru mandrams, 131
guru mantra, 45, 115
Guru Purnima, 71
guru(s), 3, 13, 43, 45, 49, 71, 81, 107, 109, 115, 117, 119, 121, 131, 133, 147, 153
half-converted, 139
hatha, 45, 55
hatha yoga, 55
headshaving, 99
healing, 55
health, vi, xi, 17, 55, 57, 59, 135, 165
heroin, 57
Himalayan Academy, i-ii
Hindu Catechism and Creed, 27
Hindu(s), ii, 27, 39, 49, 81, 85, 99, 111, 125, 127, 139, 149
Hinduism, i-ii, x, 125
Holy Bible, 27
hospitality, vi, 95
householder, 61, 69, 97, 159, 163
humility, 23, 147
hymns, 27, 133
immanent, 29, 33
immortality, 63
impropriety, xiii
incarnation, 121
incognito, 157
income, 69, 71, 83
independence, 101, 105
independent, 101, 163
India, 61, 131
Indian, 39, 53, 123, 155
indomitable, 5, 73
infiltrate, 127, 149

initiate, 119
initiates, 161
initiation, 115, 117, 137, 157
injustices, 5
insect(s), xiii, 3, 17
instinct, 9, 15
instinctive, 9
instinctive-intellectual, 153
interfaith, vii, 125
international, 19
interracial, 19
intimacy, 103
intimate, 85, 163
intrinsic evil, 33
Iraivan, 37, 47, 131
ivory, 19
Jai, 23
japa, 45
jealousy, 9, 45
jewelry, 85, 89
job, 101
justice, 31, 73, 75
Kadaitswami, 167
Kailasa Parampara, iii, 167
Kali Yuga, ix
karma(s), v, 5, 21, 31, 33, 45, 57, 63, 151
karma yoga, 45
Kauai Aadheenam, 47, 131
Kauai, 37, 47, 131
kavadi, 47
kill, 15, 17
kindness, 99
kiss, 109
Kumbalavalai, 37
kundalini, 45, 147
language(s), x, xii, 15, 19, 39
leaders, 105, 125
learning, 3, 7, 37, 39, 41, 121, 131
leavings, 115
lectures, xii
liberal hindus, 127
Liberation, 3, 33, 63, 127, 167
libraries, 137
life readings, 43
lineage, 13, 27, 37, 69, 71, 107, 111, 121, 125, 127, 137, 143, 165
lingam, 37
longevity, 57
Lord Ganesha, 31, 37
Lord Muruga, 31, 37
Lord Subramaniam Shastras, 27
lottery, 23
love-offering, 71
lucid dreaming, 43
lust, 11, 21, 81
Madurai, 37
magic, 43
magical, 147
Maha Sivaratri, 47
Mahadeva(s), 29, 31, 43
maharishi, xiii
mahasamadhi, xii
mandrams, 131
Manikkavasagar, 27
mantra(s), v, 13, 33, 45, 49, 63, 115
marriage(s), vi, xi, 11, 83, 85, 87, 89, 91, 97, 99, 103, 107, 109, 111
married women, 87, 97
materialist, 127
maya, 31
mead, 59
mealtimes, 87
meat, 11, 55
medical, 55, 77
medicine, 53
meditation, 5, 13, 39, 41, 45, 47, 109, 115
mediumship, 43
Meenakshi, 37
meetings, xiii, 49, 133
member(s), 83, 91, 105, 111, 123, 125, 135, 137, 157
memberships, 139
mendicants, 61, 155
menses, 85
mentors, 43
microbe, 17
milk, 137
mind-reading, 43
ministry, 157
minorities, 75
mission house, 133
mission(s), vii, 37, 43, 71, 131, 133, 149
missionaries, 73
Moksha, 33
monastery(s), vii, 91, 95, 135, 137, 143, 147, 155, 157
money, vi, xi, 23, 71, 95, 101, 121, 135, 153
monistic, 29
monistic theism, 29
mors voluntaria religiosa, 15
mountaintop perspective, 9
mridangam, 39
Muruga, 31, 37, 47, 131
music, 21, 39, 57, 95, 99
namaskaram, 49
namaste, 49
name-giving, 99
Nandinatha, i-iii, xi, xiii, 27, 127, 163, 165, 167
Nataraja, 37
Natchintanai, 27, 133
natha(s), 27, 165
Natha Yoga Sutras, 27
nation, 17, 73
naturopathy, 55
nicotine, 57
niyamas, v, 13
nondualism, 29
non-hindu, 49, 111

nonownership, 159
nonstealing, 11
nontouching, 161
nonviolence, 15
obedience, 105, 147
occultism, v, 43
occupation, 83
offend, 19, 105
offer, 23, 39, 47, 49, 57, 65, 115, 117, 119, 121
opposition, 73
ordained, xii
orphanages, 61
orthodoxy, 163
ostracize, 99, 141
outsider, 141
palmists, 43
Panchakshara, 33
parartha puja, 37, 159
Parasivam, iii, 29, 33, 49, 115
parliamentarians, vi, 75
partnership(s), 107, 109, 135
Patanjali, 27
patriotic, 73
peers, 59, 105
penance, 13, 47, 117
pendant, 87, 89
pests, 17
philosophy(s), 29, 139
physician, 57
pilgrimage, 7, 37, 131, 157
pillars, 149
planet, 7
politics, vi, xi, 73, 149, 161
pornography, 15
possessions, 155
poverty, 69
power of affirmation, 41
pray, 39, 43, 63, 143
preach, 7, 29
preceptor, 3, 43, 59, 77, 141, 143
precepts, 167, x
predators, 17, 73
pregnancy, 59
prideful postures, 23
priesthood, vii, 131
priests, 131
Primal Soul, 29
Primal Substance, 29
probationary year, 137
profession(s), 23, 73, 83, 87, 103
professional, 23, 83, 87
progeny, 143
promiscuity, 23, 81
prostrate, 115, 121
protocol, vii, x-xiii, 39, 113, 115, 117, 119, 121, 123, 125, 127, 157, 161
psychedelics, 57
psychic, 43
puberty, 99, 103
puja, 37, 159
Pure Consciousness, 29
quantum level, 55
rebellion, 101
recitation, 13
reconcile, ix, 63, 71, 141, 151
reincarnation, 33, 147
relatives, 97, 123
religious solitaire, 61
remarry, 89, 111
remorse, xiii, 13, 109, 141
renunciate(s), 89, 121
renunciation, 11, 21, 61, 89, 105, 121, 147, 159
reptile(s), ix, 3, 19
respected elder, 61
restaurants, 157
retirement, 61, 69
revolution, 73
rice, 47
rishi, 27, 163
rites, 39, 65, 89, 99, 107, 123, 163
ritual(s), 13, 39, 71, 109
rudraksha(s), 13, 49, 89
sacraments, 7, 99, 131, 133
sadhaka(s), xi, 121, 123, 147, 151
saffron robes, 121, 163
Sage Yogaswami, iii, x, 27, 133
Saiva atmartha puja, 37
Saiva Dharma Shastras, 133, 167
Saiva dharmasala(s), 131
Saiva, ii, 27, 29, 33, 37, 85, 127, 131, 133, 137, 139, 167
Saiva Siddhanta, 29, 33, 127, 137
Saiva Siddhanta Yoga Order, 137, ii
Saivism, 33, 139, 149, vii
Saivite(s), 27, 39, 49, 111, 131, 133, 139
Saktas, 125
salutations to the sun, 55
samadhi, 41, iii
Sambandar, 27
sampradaya, 163
Sanatana Dharma, 149
sandalpaste, 89
sandals, 115
sannyas, 91
sannyasin(s), 61
Sanskrit, 39, xii
Satguru, iii, vii, x-xi, 3, 33, 43, 47, 71, 89, 91, 107, 115, 117, 119, 121, 123, 131, 133, 139, 143, 147, 167
satsang, 133
scholarships, 71
scientist(s), vi, 77
scripture(s), v, ix, 13, 27, 75, 125, 149, 167

secret(s), 21, 33, 77, 117
secular humanist, 127
secular, 7, 127, 161
self-effacement, 153
self-erasement, 153
sepulcher(s), 37
sex, 11, 19, 21, 23, 89, 103, 109, 123, 153, 159
sexual fantasy, 21, 159
shanti mantra, 49
shastras, 27, 133, 167
Shum, 39
shun, 111, 141
Siddhanta, ii, 29, 33, 127, 137
sing, 39, 133
Siva's money, 71
Siva-Sakti, 29, 31
Sivachariya, 131
Sivaratri, 47
Sivaya, 49, i-ii
skill(s), 39, 99, 103
slander, 15, 119
Smarta Dasanami orders, 163
Smarta(s), 125, 163
smoke, 57
song(s), 21, 27, 133
steadfastness, 11
steal, 109
study, v, xii, 7, 13, 29, 39, 41, 45, 127, 137, 143, 155
subsuperconscious, 41
subconscious, ix, 41
subjugate, 77
Subramuniyaswami, i-ii
substratum, 29
subtle bodies, 41
successors, 121, 165
Suddha Saiva Siddhanta, 29
suicide, 15
Sundarar, 27
sunrise, 45
sunshine, 47
swami, xii, 91, 121, 123, 153
swimming, 55
symbols, v, 49
tambura, 39
Tamil, xii, 27
tastes, 53
taxes, 69
teach, 37, 61, 103, 137, 149, 159
teachings, 13, 27, 41, 63, 127
television, 21
temperance, 59
temple builders, 131
temple(s), v, vii, 31, 33, 37, 47, 71, 85, 123, 131, 133, 135, 149, 157, 159
tenets, 75, 85
terminal illness, 15
terminally ill, 63
Thayumanavar, 27
theism, 29
three pillars, 149
Tirukural, 27
Tirumantiram, 27
Tirumular, 27
Tirunandi, xxxii
Tiruvadi, 37, 47
Tiruvalluvar, 27
tithing, 13, 71
tobacco, 57, vi
tolerance, x
tortoise, 19
tradition(s), x, 3, 15, 21, 27, 37, 39, 43, 71, 81, 85, 87, 89, 91, 99, 103, 105, 109, 111, 119, 121, 125, 155, 157, 161, 163
trance mediumship, 43
trance(s), 43
transcendent, 33
transcends, 29
transmute, 89, 109
travel, 39, 155, 157, vii
tree(s), 3, 19
trespasser, 119
truthfulness, 11
Tyaf, 39
unanimous agreement, 133
unfoldment, 119, 123
unmarried, 91, 101
unprovocative, 89
unscrupulous, 77
Upanishads, 27
Vaishnavas, 125
vanakkam, 49
Vedanta, 29
Vedas, 27
Vedic-Agamic, 27
veena, 39, 95
vegetarian, 55
Vel of Grace, 31
venerate, 95, 121
vigil, 63
vilify, 125
violence, xi, 15, 21
virgin, 91
vote(s), 133, 161
vow(s), 11, 13, 71, 91, 103, 141, 147, 149, 159, 167
water(s), xiii, 53, 115
wealth, vi, 3, 69, 71, 73, 149, 165, 167
wedding pendant, 87
wedding(s), 87, 107, 163
widows, vi, xi, 83, 87, 89
wines, 59
wool, 155
worthy, 143
yamas, v, 11
yoga(s), ii, v, 7, 27, 33, 45, 55, 89, 137, 147, 151
Yoga Sutras, 27
Yogaswami, iii, x, 27, 133

Colophon

LIVING WITH SIVA, HINDUISM'S NANDINATHA SUTRAS, WAS DESIGNED, ILLUSTRATED AND TYPESET BY THE SWAMIS OF THE SAIVA SIDdhanta Yoga Order at Kauai's Hindu Monastery on Hawaii's Garden Island. This fourth book in the Rishi Collection was composed on a Macintosh Portable and assembled on a network of Macintosh II's using Microsoft Word and QuarkXpress with its various extensions, including Sonar Bookends for indexing. The text was laser set in Adobe's Minion family of fonts, the sutras themselves in 12.5-point medium with 15-point linespacing. The seventy-three Rajput paintings were reproduced conventionally by LithoColor of Honolulu, Hawaii, using a 120-line screen. The twelve patterned graphics were produced using Adobe's Streamline and Illustrator software and a Wacom graphics tablet, then output directly to negatives at 1270 dpi on a Linotron Imagesetter. The cover was ported to a Scitex for output on a high-resolution color plotter. The book was printed in Harrisonburg, Virginia, by Banta Company on a Timson web-offset press using 55# Butte des Morts, a predominantly recycled paper. The cover art, portraying many of the aspects of Hindu life that this book explains, was painted in 1810 in India. Renowned San Francisco artist John Kuzich designed the cover and the Himalayan Academy logo. The back cover photo of His Holiness Sivaya Subramuniyaswami was taken by Rohini Kumar at his national studios in Kuala Lumpur, Malaysia.

Related Publications From Himalayan Academy

Dancing with Siva

Created for those wishing to understand the Hindu path and wisdom, *Dancing with Siva* is written in the catechism style of questions and answers, explaining the spiritual beliefs and steps to enlightenment of the world's oldest living spiritual system. Beautifully crafted and illustrated insights about karma, reincarnation, yoga, nonviolence and God's presence in all things.

Hinduism Today

"Affirming the dharma and recording the modern history of nearly a billion Hindus" is the bold motto of this graphically rich monthly newspaper. Hinduism Today is an award-winning, computer-produced information resource reaching thirty-three countries. Nearly one hundred articles/items in every issue cover the events, people, issues, lifestyles, arts and metaphysical wisdom of global Hinduism.

Passing on the Power

In Hinduism the light and knowledge attained by a God-Realized master is transmitted through initiation to his successor. These six Satgurus are inheritors of the Kailasa Parampara and Nandinatha Sampradaya, a Saivite lineage teaching monistic theism. In this calligraphic masterpiece the artist has scribed thousands of mantras in colored inks with a quill. 8½" by 11."

Order Form

All prices are listed in U.S. currency. When ordering, specify name of item, quantity and unit prices. Add 10% for postage and handling in USA and 20% foreign, $1.50 minimum. Foreign orders are shipped sea mail unless otherwise specified and additional postage is provided. (Add 50% for foreign airmail postage.)

☐ *Yes, I would like to receive a free literature packet.*

☐ *Yes, I would like to subscribe to Hinduism Today.*

☐ 1-year subscription $24 ☐ 2-year subscription $36

I would also like to order the following items:

☐ *Dancing with Siva* $9.95 ☐ *Living with Siva* $8.95

☐ *Passing on the Power* (Poster art) $1.95

____

____

☐ My payment is enclosed. Charge to: ☐ Master Card ☐ Visa

Card number: ______________________________

Expiration date: ______________ Total of purchase: __________

Signature: ______________________________

____

First and Last Name (Please Print) Telephone

____

Address

____

____

Mail orders to Himalayan Academy Publications, P.O. Box 157, Hanamaulu, Hawaii USA 96715

These publications are also available in Malaysia and Mauritius. For prices, write to: Siddhanta Publications, P.O. Box 301, 46730 Petaling Jaya, Selangor, Malaysia or Himalayan Academy Publications, La Pointe, Riviere du Rempart, Mauritius.